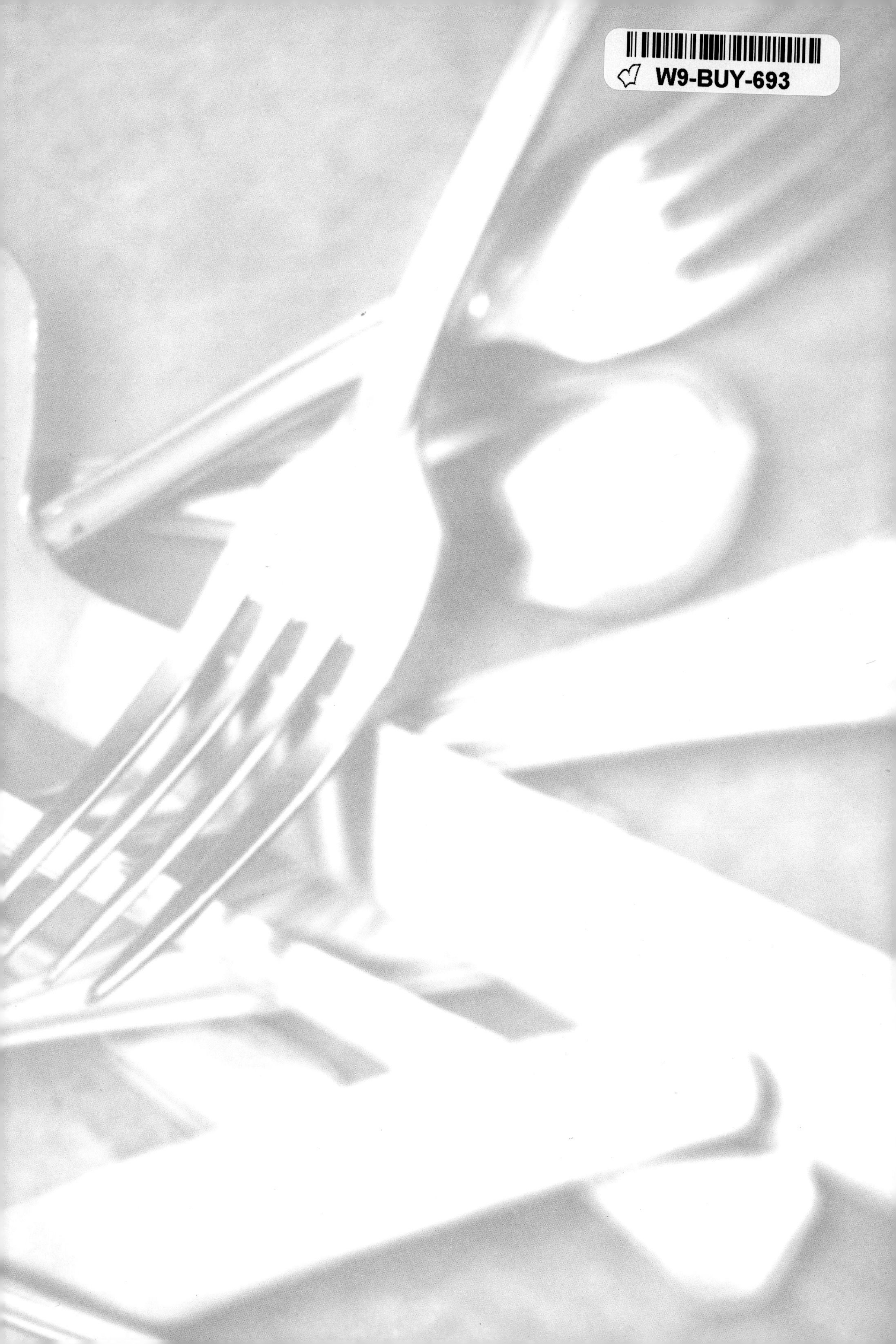

72 Market St.

Dishes It Out!

Tony Bill, Roland Gibert, and Dudley Moore
photographed by Danny Duchovny

72 Market St.

a collection of recipes and portraits
Dishes. It. Out!
from a classic Venice restaurant

by ROLAND GIBERT
with ROBERT LIA

Ten Speed Press
Berkeley, California

TEN SPEED PRESS
P.O. BOX 7123
BERKELEY, CALIFORNIA 94707
WWW.TENSPEED.COM

DISTRIBUTED IN CANADA BY TEN SPEED PRESS CANADA, IN NEW ZEALAND BY TANDEM PRESS, IN AUSTRALIA BY SIMON AND
SCHUSTER AUSTRALIA, IN SOUTH AFRICA BY REAL BOOKS, IN SINGAPORE AND MALAYSIA BY BERKELEY BOOKS, AND IN THE UNITED
KINGDOM AND EUROPE BY AIRLIFT BOOKS.

DESIGN BY SARGENT & BERMAN, INC.

LIBRARY OF CONGRESS CATALOGING-IN-PUBLICATION DATA

GIBERT, ROLAND 1948-
72 MARKET ST. DISHES IT OUT!: A COLLECTION OF RECIPES AND PORTRAITS FROM A CLASSIC VENICE RESTAURANT / BY ROLAND
GIBERT, WITH ROBERT LIA.
P. CM.
INCLUDES INDEX.
ISBN 1-58008-067-7
1. COOKERY. 2. 72 MARKET ST. OYSTER BAR AND GRILL.
3. CELEBRITIES-PORTRAITS. 4. PORTRAIT PHOTOGRAPHY. I. LIA, ROBERT, 1968- . II. TITLE.
TX714.G532   1998
641.5-DC21   97-17386
CIP

FIRST TEN SPEED PRESS EDITION, 1999
PRINTED IN HONG KONG

1 2 3 4 5 6 7 8 9 10 — 03 02 01 00 99

Table of Contents

Appetizers and Hors d'Oeuvres 11

1 Duck spring rolls with orange ginger sauce 13

Gil Borgos - On a Roll 14

2 Veal meatballs 15

3 Grilled prawns with Japanese vinaigrette 17

4 Cod fritters with rouille 19

William Turner - Ceviche on the Canal 20

5 Ceviche 21

Steve Wallace - Vintage Wally 22

6 House-cured salmon with sauerkraut 23

7 Onion and Cheddar cheese tart 25

8 Artichoke and asparagus terrine with beet vinaigrette 26

9 Dungeness crab and crispy noodle galette with spiced mustard sauce 29

The Honorable Matt Fong and Paula Fong - Party Politics 30

10 Crab cakes with beluga caviar 31

Seymour Cassel - Up in Smoke 32

11 Chicken satay with peanut dipping sauce 33

Salads 35

Katherine Bonner - The Little Mermaid 36

12 Crayfish salad wrapped in smoked salmon with mango vinaigrette 37

Connie Linn - In Living Color 38

13 Maine lobster napoleon with mango vinaigrette 39

14 Warm pear and roquefort torte with salad greens and red wine vinaigrette .. 40

15 Grilled seafood and vegetable salad with lemon vinaigrette 43

Nancy Kay and E.F. Kitchen with Boris and Igor - Photo Op 44

16 Calamari salad 45

Aleiza and Lysandra - Chopstix 46

17 Chinese chicken salad 47

Peter Alexander - Lunch in the Abstract 48

18 Grilled portobello mushrooms and a small mesclun with red bell pepper vinaigrette .. 49

David Baerwald - After Hours 50

19 Fall fruit salad 51

Soups 53

Mary Steenburgen and Ted Danson - Soup du Jour 54

20 Spicy corn chowder 55

21 Seafood gumbo with rock shrimp 56

22 Lobster bisque 57

23 Mushroom bisque 58

24 Black bean soup 59

Sharon Jacobucci and Leslie Bisno - Meal Ticket 60

25	VEGETABLE SPLIT PEA SOUP	61
	Wendy Al and Billy Al Bengston - The First Time I Ever Liked Gazpacho	62
26	GAZPACHO	63
27	SWEET POTATO CLAM CHOWDER	64
28	CREAM OF PARSNIP SOUP WITH GINGER	65

Vegetables 67

	Robert Graham - Self-Portrait in Mashed Potatoes	68
29	72 MARKET ST. MASHED POTATOES	69
30	POTATOES AU GRATIN	70
31	CELERY ROOT MOUSSE	71
32	EGGPLANT AND BELL PEPPER TERRINE WITH SUN-DRIED TOMATO VINAIGRETTE	72
33	WARM ASPARAGUS WITH CARROT TARRAGON DRESSING	75
	Sharon Truax and Derrik Van Nimwegen - Say Ahhh!	76
34	FENNEL RATATOUILLE	77

Risotto and Pasta 79

35	VEGETABLE RISOTTO	80
36	SEAFOOD RISOTTO WITH SAFFRON	81
	James Evans and Daniel Samakow - Your Place or Ours?	82
37	BANANA SQUASH RAVIOLI	83
38	LOBSTER AND GREEN ONION RAVIOLI WITH HERB SAUCE	85
	Dudley Moore - Hitting the High Notes	86
39	FARFALLE WITH FAVA BEANS AND MUSHROOM RAGOUT	87
40	FETTUCCINE WITH GRILLED CHICKEN AND VEGETABLES AND RED BELL PEPPER PESTO	89
	Alexandra Keller - The Shortest Distance Between Two Points Is a Straight Line	90
41	SWISS CHARD GNOCCHI WITH SAGE BUTTER	91

Fish 93

	Robert Fegan - Catch of the day	94
42	GRILLED SALMON WITH DIJON AND POMMERY MUSTARD SAUCE	95
	Ed Moses - In Rare Form	96
43	CHARRED PEPPERED RARE AHI TUNA WITH SAUTÉED SPINACH AND RED ONION SOUBISE	97
44	72 MARKET ST. BOUILLABAISSE	98
	Nate and Judy Chroman and Marjorie Katz - The Last Supper	100
45	SEARED SEA SCALLOPS WITH CARAMELIZED ONIONS AND SWEET AND SOUR SAUCE	101
46	BAKED HALIBUT WITH WILD MUSHROOM CRUST AND LENTIL RAGOUT	102
	Joe DeAngelis - Pumping Paella	104
47	72 MARKET ST. PAELLA	105
	Linda Stewart and Danny Duchovny - Two Shot	106
48	72 MARKET ST. PAPILLOTE	107

Fowl 109

| | *Helena Kallianiotes- Zesty* | 110 |
| 49 | GRILLED MARINATED CHICKEN WITH TOMATILLO SALSA | 111 |

Steve Ferguson - Concerto for Chicken and Apples......112

50 CHICKEN WITH CARAMELIZED APPLES AND CALVADOS......113

Helen Bartlett and Tony Bill - Fowl Play......114

51 CHICKEN STUFFED WITH TARRAGON MOUSSE IN A SEA URCHIN SAUCE......115

52 ROASTED SQUAB WITH CANDIED GARLIC AND GREEN LENTIL RAGOUT......116

53 MUSCOVY DUCK WITH PORT WINE SAUCE......118

54 CRISPY AIR-DRIED DUCK WITH PEAR AND MINT SAUCE......119

Robert Lia and Canoah - Main Squeeze......120

55 ED LANDRY'S QUAIL GUMBO......121

Meat   123

Leonard Schwartz - From Market St. to Maple Dr.......122

56 72 MARKET ST. MEAT LOAF AND GRAVY......125

57 72 MARKET ST. KICK ASS CHILI AND CORN MUFFINS......127

Kicking Ass at the Art Walk......128

58 OSSO BUCO......129

Andy Nevill and Mark Steffen - Tattoo To Go......130

59 VEAL CHOP WITH PORCINI MUSHROOMS AND SWEET POTATO PURÉE......131

60 SWEETBREAD AND LOBSTER CHARTREUSE WITH PEA COULIS......132

Bear - I've got a bone to pick. 134

61 GRILLED PORK CHOP WITH TOMATO GINGER CHUTNEY......135

62 ROASTED RACK OF LAMB WITH ORANGE AND JUNIPER BERRY CRUST......136

Desserts   139

Julie Gibert - Sweet Dreams......140

63 APPLE GALETTE WITH CARAMEL SAUCE......141

64 VENICE BANANA NAPOLEON......142

Roy Doumani - Why Men Have Mustaches......144

65 72 MARKET ST. BROWNIES......145

Carol Doumani - Dressed to Spill......146

66 CHOCOLATE HAZELNUT TORTE......147

67 PECAN PIE......149

David Vostmyer, Peter Sargent, and Greg Berman - Just Desserts......150

68 CHOCOLATE CRÈME CARAMEL......151

69 LEMON MERINGUE TART......153

Michael Schiffer - Chow Hound......154

70 CHEESECAKE WITH RASPBERRY COULIS......155

Robert Lia - Food for Thought......156

71 SUMMER PUDDING......157

72 CHOCOLATE "BOMBE"......158

Roland Gibert - Bombe Scare......160

Index   161

ACKNOWLEDGMENTS......164

Tip Not Included......167

When I came to 72 Market St. Oyster Bar and Grill in January of 1994, the restaurant was already a Los Angeles institution. Conceived in the early '80s by filmmaker Tony Bill and entertainer Dudley Moore as a beach bistro where they could enjoy fine food and relax with friends, it quickly become known for its superb American cuisine, friendly service, and comfortable atmosphere. Dudley and other musicians entertained nightly, playing to an SRO crowd, which came as much to people-watch as to devour Chef Leonard Schwartz's meat loaf and kick ass chili.

Drawing inspiration from the eclectic Venice neighborhood, as well as from the eccentric mix of creative people who became regular patrons, over the past fourteen years the restaurant has developed a rich and unique personality. What seems to set 72 Market St. apart from many Los Angeles restaurants established in the '80s is the fact that the food and the atmosphere are familiar and comfortable, a return to American home cooking with no pretensions, just impeccable preparation and presentation.

As you can imagine, when customers who had patronized the restaurant for more than a decade learned that a French chef was joining the 72 Market St. family, they were skeptical. The restaurant had always been so quintessentially American, whereas my signature dishes at Tulipe, a restaurant I founded in 1989 with Maurice Peguet, included pigs' trotters stuffed with escargot and a sweetbread and lobster chartreuse. Would such dishes replace the famous kick ass chili and the grilled chicken with tomatillo salsa, they must have wondered? What about the mashed potatoes and the meat loaf, to say nothing of the 72 Market St. brownie?

But the patrons of the restaurant did not have to worry. While I am a classically trained French chef, and some of the dishes I enjoy preparing might seem unusual to an American with a palate for home-cooked dishes, my greatest pleasure is to cook a broad spectrum of foods, to satisfy the tastes of every guest. For those diners who are adventurous eaters, my Chef de Cuisine Robert Lia and I are pleased to prepare dishes which invigorate the palate, ranging from seafood en papillote to Muscovy duck. But we are also delighted to serve 72's traditional crab cakes, grilled chicken, and pecan pie, because we want to offer our guests the food they have come to identify with 72 Market St. Thus, our menu blends the old and the new. Diners can count on being able to order charred rare ahi tuna, but from our nightly specials they may also choose cod fritters or a crayfish salad wrapped in smoked salmon.

With this cookbook we offer you the opportunity to recreate some of our best-loved dishes in your home kitchen. On the following pages you will find a collection of recipes that we feel capture the flavor of Venice and the tastes of our very creative clientele. And as illustration, we have invited many of 72's friends and patrons to pose for portraits with their favorite dishes. These photographs have been taken by thirteen of the finest photographers in town, all part of the restaurant's extended family. Putting the book together has been a community effort, and we are thankful to everyone who contributed.

Will the chili you prepare from the recipe in this book taste exactly the same in your home as it does in the restaurant? Will the mashed potatoes be as fluffy? Perhaps, but perhaps not. Even when master chefs use the same recipes, the finished dishes are not identical, because cooking is an art, a reflection of the personal style of the chef. The quantities, oven temperatures, and kitchen utensils we have specified are only suggestions. You may have an allergy to garlic, your oven may cook hotter than ours, or you may not own a blender. Don't let these things stop you from trying a recipe. Your subtle variations of method or amount will make each dish unique. We have left room on each page for you to make notes and record special touches. I encourage you to use our recipes as your guide, but be creative — that is what cooking is all about!

A few words of advice: Let the product decide the menu. If the recipe calls for salmon, but the salmon you find in your market is frozen, instead, select a fresh fish or a different recipe to prepare. Buy what's in season; wait until October to try the fall fruit salad, and cook the spicy corn chowder in August, when you can purchase fresh ears of corn from a roadside stand. Also, if you are planning to cook one of these dishes for a party, I suggest you try it ahead of time, both to avoid last minute-crises, and also because in trying it, you may find ways to adapt it to your own style and kitchen.

Robert Lia and I, and the rest of the staff sincerely hope you will enjoy preparing your favorite dishes from 72 Market St. in your own kitchen, and that through cooking them, you will make them your own. Bonne chance and bon appétit!

Roland Gibert

FOR QUESTIONS, COMMENTS, OR HELP WITH THE FOLLOWING RECIPES,
WE INVITE YOU TO VISIT OUR WEBSITE AT

HTTP://WWW.72MARKETST.COM

OR E-MAIL US AT
COOKBOOK@72MARKETST.COM

Roland Gibert
photographed by Plaridel Atil

Appetizers and Hors d'Oeuvres

1 Duck Spring Rolls with
Orange Ginger Sauce..13

Gil Borgos, "On a Roll"..14

2 Veal Meatballs...15

3 Grilled Prawns with Japanese Vinaigrette....................17

4 Cod Fritters with Rouille.......................................19

William Turner, "Ceviche on the Canal"......................20

5 Ceviche..21

Steve Wallace, "Vintage Wally"..............................22

6 House-Cured Salmon with Sauerkraut......................23

7 Onion and Cheddar Cheese Tart.............................25

8 Artichoke and Asparagus Terrine with
Beet Vinaigrette..26

9 Dungeness Crab and Crispy Noodle Galette
with Spiced Mustard Sauce.......................................29

*The Honorable Matt Fong and Paula Fong,
"Party Politics"*..30

10 Crab Cakes with Beluga Caviar.............................31

Seymour Cassel, "Up in Smoke"............................32

11 Chicken Satay with Peanut Dipping Sauce.............33

Orange Ginger Sauce

¹/₄ CUP CHOPPED SHALLOTS

2 TABLESPOONS CHOPPED FRESH GINGER

1 ¹/₂ TEASPOONS BUTTER

¹/₂ CUP PLUM WINE

2 CUPS FRESH ORANGE JUICE

¹/₂ CUP WHIPPING CREAM

1 TEASPOON ARROWROOT

¹/₂ TEASPOON COLD WATER

1 In a saucepan, sweat the shallots and ginger in the butter over medium heat for 3 minutes, or until the vegetables are tender.

2 Add the plum wine and cook over medium heat until the liquid is reduced in half.

3 Add the orange juice and continue to cook over medium heat until the liquid is again reduced in half.

4 Add the cream and bring the sauce to a boil. Reduce the heat to low. Mix the arrowroot with the water and stir into sauce to thicken. The sauce should be thick enough to coat the back of a spoon.

5 Serve warm. You may prepare the sauce up to one day ahead and reheat before serving.

Serving Size: 6

Duck Spring Rolls
with Orange Ginger Sauce

¹/₄ YELLOW SQUASH, PEEL ONLY

¹/₄ ZUCCHINI, PEEL ONLY

³/₄ TEASPOON SESAME OIL

³/₄ TEASPOON PEANUT OIL

¹/₄ CUP SLICED BROCCOLI

¹/₄ MEDIUM RED ONION, SLICED

2 CELERY STALKS, SLICED DIAGONALLY

¹/₃ RED BELL PEPPER, SLICED

¹/₃ YELLOW BELL PEPPER, SLICED

¹/₃ GREEN BELL PEPPER, SLICED

¹/₄ FENNEL BULB, SLICED

SALT AND PEPPER

1 POUND ROASTED AIR-DRIED DUCK
MEAT, WITH SKIN ON

6 LARGE EGG ROLL SKINS

1 EGG YOLK, BEATEN

PEANUT OIL FOR FRYING

ORANGE GINGER SAUCE
(SEE RECIPE ON FACING PAGE)

1 Using a vegetable peeler, strip off the peel from the yellow squash and zucchini, then cut into julienne. Heat the sesame oil and peanut oil in a wok or a large sauté pan. Add the yellow squash and zucchini peels, broccoli, red onion, celery, red bell pepper, yellow bell pepper, green bell pepper, and fennel to the heated oil, and sauté until tender, about 4 minutes. (To simplify the recipe you may use green bell pepper in place of the yellow and red bell pepper). Season with salt and pepper to taste.

2 Finely dice the cooked duck meat and add to the vegetable mixture.

3 Divide the filling evenly into 6 portions and spoon onto egg roll skins. Fold over one corner of the skin to cover the filling. Then fold over the right and left sides to form an envelope. Brush the top with the beaten egg and roll upward from the bottom to seal. Roll tightly and neatly, making sure that all the filling is sealed securely in the wrapper.

4 Heat the peanut oil in a deep fryer or wok. It is necessary to use enough oil to cover the spring rolls so they will steam from the inside. Cook for 3 to 5 minutes, until golden brown, pushing them down into the oil if they float. When they are done, drain on paper towels to remove excess oil.

5 To serve, cut each roll diagonally into two wedge-shaped pieces and serve with Orange Ginger Sauce for dipping.

Serving Size: 6

Gil Borgos, The Greeter - "On a Roll"
DUCK SPRING ROLLS WITH ORANGE GINGER SAUCE
photographed by Pablo Aguilar

Veal Meatballs

2 1/2 POUNDS GROUND VEAL

3/4 CUP PREPARED BREADCRUMBS

1/4 CUP WHITE WINE

2 EGGS

1 1/2 TABLESPOONS MINCED CHIVES

1 1/2 TABLESPOONS CHOPPED PARSLEY

1 TABLESPOON CHOPPED SHALLOT

1 1/2 TEASPOONS CHOPPED CHERVIL

1 1/2 TEASPOONS CHOPPED TARRAGON

1 TABLESPOON RED PEPPER FLAKES

SALT AND PEPPER

1. Preheat the oven to 350 degrees.

2. In a large mixing bowl or electric mixer, combine veal, breadcrumbs, wine, eggs, chives, parsley, shallot, chervil, tarragon, red pepper flakes, and salt and pepper to taste. Mix until well incorporated.

3. Roll into balls about the size of a walnut, one ounce each.

4. Place the meatballs in a greased roasting pan and cook until golden, about 5 to 8 minutes.

Serving Size: 36 small meatballs

Japanese Vinaigrette

3 TABLESPOONS CHOPPED FRESH GINGER

1 SHALLOT, CHOPPED

2 TABLESPOONS PREPARED HORSERADISH

1 1/2 TEASPOONS CHOPPED GARLIC

1 1/2 TEASPOONS CHOPPED ONION

1/4 CUP BROWN SUGAR, PACKED

3/4 TEASPOON WASABI PASTE

3 TABLESPOONS LEMON JUICE

3 TABLESPOONS LIME JUICE

1/4 CUP SOY SAUCE

1/4 CUP RICE VINEGAR

1 1/2 CUPS PEANUT OIL

2 TABLESPOONS SESAME OIL

SALT AND PEPPER

1. In a blender, combine the ginger, shallot, horseradish, garlic, onion, brown sugar, and wasabi.

2. Add the lemon and lime juices, soy sauce, and rice vinegar and blend on medium speed for 4 minutes, until smooth.

3. With the motor running, slowly add the peanut oil and sesame oil.

4. Season with salt and pepper to taste. Chill until ready to serve.

Serving Size: 6

What could be simpler than throwing a few shrimp on the grill? The vinaigrette provides a subtle finish that enhances the flavor of the charred shellfish. To prevent the prawns from sticking to the grill, rub it lightly with an oiled rag before heating.

Grilled Prawns
with Japanese Vinaigrette

18 JUMBO SHRIMP, PEELED AND DEVEINED

1 TEASPOON OLIVE OIL

SALT AND PEPPER

JAPANESE VINAIGRETTE
(SEE RECIPE ON FACING PAGE)

2 TABLESPOONS CHOPPED CHIVES

1 Heat the barbecue grill. Rub the shrimp with oil and season with salt and pepper to taste.

2 Grill the shrimp over high heat until they are firm and opaque, about 3 to 5 minutes. Split with a knife to check for doneness if you are unsure.

3 Drizzle with Japanese Vinaigrette, and serve warm, garnished with chopped chives.

Serving Size: 6

If the sauce breaks, put a small portion of it into another bowl and add a few drops of
water. Whisk, adding more water, a little at a time, until the sauce comes together.
Rouille
Gradually add the rest of the Rouille to the new bowl, whisking constantly.

1 1/2 TEASPOONS CHOPPED GARLIC

PINCH OF SAFFRON

A FEW DROPS OF EXTRA VIRGIN OLIVE OIL

1/3 CUP OF A WHOLE BAKED POTATO, SKINNED

1 EGG YOLK

3/4 TEASPOON DIJON MUSTARD

1/2 CUP EXTRA VIRGIN OLIVE OIL

PINCH OF CAYENNE PEPPER

SALT

1. Combine the chopped garlic and saffron in a blender with a few drops of the oil and blend until puréed.

2. Add the potato, egg yolk, and mustard, and blend.

3. While the motor is running, gradually add the rest of the oil.

4. Season with cayenne pepper and salt.

5. Serve at room temperature.

Serving Size: 6

Cod Fritters with Rouille

7 OUNCES SALT COD

1 CUP WATER

1 1/2 TEASPOONS BUTTER

1 1/2 TEASPOONS CHOPPED GARLIC

1 TEASPOON RED PEPPER FLAKES

7/8 CUP ALL-PURPOSE FLOUR

3 EGGS

1 1/2 TEASPOONS CHOPPED PARSLEY

SALT AND PEPPER

PEANUT OIL FOR FRYING

1. Place the soaked or rinsed cod in a saucepan with enough water to cover, and bring to a boil. Reduce the heat to low and simmer. If cod was soaked overnight, cook for 10 minutes, uncovered. If cod was rinsed prior to cooking, cook for 45 minutes, uncovered. Strain and discard the liquid.

2. In a medium saucepan, bring 1 cup of water to a boil and add the butter, chopped garlic, and red pepper flakes. Bring to a boil and remove from heat.

3. Gradually add the flour. Mix with a spoon until ingredients are well incorporated and form a dough-like ball.

4. Transfer the mixture to the bowl of an electric mixer. Beat on medium speed, using a paddle attachment if you have one, and add the eggs one at a time.

5. Add the salt cod and parsley and mix until combined. Season with salt and pepper. Chill until ready to use.

6. Heat the oil in a deep fryer or saucepan. Using an ice cream scoop or a tablespoon, drop rounded portions of the cod mixture (about 1 tablespoon each) into the hot oil, and deep fry until golden brown. Serve with Rouille.

Serving Size: 6

William Turner, Gallery Owner – "Ceviche on the Canal"
CEVICHE
photographed by Michael Cullen

Ceviche is a dish of raw seafood that has been marinated in lime juice, herbs and aromatic vegetables for several hours, tenderizing the flesh of the fish and turning it from translucent to white. For a cocktail party, skewer whole bay scallops and pieces of sea bass for easier handling.

Ceviche

1 POUND BAY SCALLOPS (ABOUT 2 CUPS)

1 POUND SEA BASS (ABOUT 2 CUPS)

1 1/2 CUPS FRESH LIME JUICE
(12 TO 14 LIMES)

5 ROMA TOMATOES

1 MEDIUM ONION

1/2 BUNCH CILANTRO

1/2 BUNCH OREGANO

SHREDDED LETTUCE

1 Slice the bay scallops in half. Debone the sea bass and cut into pieces the same size as the scallops.

2 Arrange the scallops and sea bass in a shallow dish and pour the lime juice over. Cover and refrigerate for 2 to 4 hours, or until no longer opaque. Drain, and discard the lime juice.

3 Peel, seed, and dice the tomatoes. Chop the onion, cilantro, and oregano.

4 When the fish has finished marinating, mix together with tomatoes, onion, cilantro and oregano. Chill and serve on a bed of shredded lettuce.

Serving Size: 6

Steve Wallace, Wine Merchant - "Vintage Wally"
HOUSE-CURED SALMON WITH SAUERKRAUT
photographed by Pablo Aguilar

This dish is simple to prepare, but you must plan ahead because the curing time is 72 hours.
Once the salmon is fully cured, it will keep for two weeks in the refrigerator or indefinitely
in the freezer, if tightly wrapped in plastic.

House-Cured Salmon with Sauerkraut

¹/₂ CUP GRANULATED SUGAR

¹/₂ CUP SALT

¹/₄ CUP CHOPPED FRESH DILL

4 WHITE PEPPERCORNS, CRACKED

1 TABLESPOON BRANDY

1 POUND SALMON FILLET, WITH THE SKIN ON

1 CUP FRESH SAUERKRAUT,
OR 1 POUND CANNED

1 TABLESPOON EXTRA VIRGIN OLIVE OIL

PINCH OF PEPPER

PINCH OF CUMIN

PINCH OF ANISEED

1 TABLESPOON CHOPPED FRESH CHIVES

1. To prepare marinade, in a small bowl, combine the sugar, salt, dill, cracked peppercorns, and brandy. Mix well.

2. Trim the fat from the belly of the salmon and cut several 1-inch-long slits through the skin.

3. Place the salmon, skin side down, in a shallow dish and pour the marinade over it. Turn the salmon to coat both sides evenly, and leave in the dish with the skin side down. Cover and chill for 72 hours.

4. Every 24 hours, turn the salmon over. It will be fully cured in 72 hours.

5. To prepare the fresh sauerkraut, drain and toss with the olive oil, pepper, cumin, and aniseed. (If using canned sauerkraut, rinse well before tossing with oil and seasonings.)

6. To serve, slice salmon very thin. Garnish with the sauerkraut, and top with chopped chives.

Serving Size: 6

Tart Shells from Mauri Dough

1 CUP ALL-PURPOSE FLOUR

¹/₂ CUP SOFTENED BUTTER

DASH OF SALT

2 EGG YOLKS

3 TABLESPOONS COLD WATER

1   Lightly grease six 4-inch tart pans.

2   Place the flour in the bowl of an electric mixer. Make a well in the center and add the softened butter, salt, egg yolk, and 1 tablespoon of the water. Stir, using a paddle attachment, until the dough comes together. If the dough is too dry, add the rest of the water, 1 tablespoon at a time.

3   Wrap the dough in plastic and chill for 2 hours.

4   Preheat the oven to 375 degrees. Roll out the dough on a floured surface until 1/4-inch thick.

5   Cut into six circles, each 1 inch larger in diameter than the tart pans. Carefully transfer the dough to the pans and trim the excess.

6   Using a fork, poke holes in the bottom of the dough. Line shells with aluminum foil and a layer of beans, rice or pie weights so that the dough will not puff.

7   Bake for 20 minutes, or until golden brown. Cool.

Serving Size: 6

Onion and Cheddar Cheese Tart

TART SHELLS FROM MAURI DOUGH
(SEE RECIPE ON FACING PAGE)

4 MEDIUM ONIONS, THINLY SLICED

1 TABLESPOON BUTTER

1 TEASPOON NUTMEG

2 EGGS, LIGHTLY BEATEN

2 TABLESPOONS WHIPPING CREAM

SALT AND PEPPER

1 CUP GRATED SHARP CHEDDAR CHEESE

1. Prepare the tart shells before beginning the onion mixture.

2. Preheat the oven to 375 degrees.

3. Sauté the onions in butter over medium heat until golden brown, about 10 to 12 minutes. Cool slightly.

4. Add the nutmeg, eggs, and whipping cream to the onions and mix thoroughly. Season with salt and pepper to taste.

5. Remove the cooked tart shells from their pans and place on a cookie sheet lined with parchment paper.

6. Place one-sixth of the onion mixture in each shell and sprinkle with Cheddar cheese.

7. Bake at 375 degrees until the onion mixture has set, about 15 minutes. Serve warm.

Serving Size: 6

A visually stunning dish, good for a party because it can be prepared in advance. Canned artichoke bottoms may be substituted for the fresh, but the tarragon must be fresh. It is the nuance of flavor from the herb that gives this light and elegant dish distinction.

Artichoke and Asparagus Terrine with Beet Vinaigrette

20 ARTICHOKES, OR 3 (14-OUNCE) CANS
ARTICHOKE BOTTOMS

JUICE OF 1 LEMON

4 LARGE LEEKS

3 MEDIUM CARROTS

3 BUNCHES MEDIUM ASPARAGUS

2 TEASPOONS UNFLAVORED GELATIN

1/3 CUP WATER

1/2 BUNCH TARRAGON, CHOPPED

SALT AND PEPPER

BEET VINAIGRETTE
(SEE RECIPE ON FACING PAGE)

1. Trim and clean the artichokes. Place them in a large stockpot and cover with water. Add the lemon juice and bring to a boil. Reduce to a simmer and cook until the hearts are soft, approximately 30 minutes.

2. While artichokes are simmering, prepare the leeks. Wash and remove the torn or dirty outermost leaves. Then, being careful not to tear them, remove 10 more leaves and set them aside. In a medium saucepan, heat water to a boil and add the whole leeks and the reserved leek leaves. Cook until tender but still firm, approximately 3 minutes. Remove from the boiling water and set in a large bowl of ice water.

3. Peel carrots and slice lengthwise, 1/4-inch thick. Refill the saucepan with water and bring to a boil. Add the carrot slices and cook until tender but still firm, approximately 5 minutes. Remove from the boiling water and set in the ice water with the leeks.

4. Peel and trim the asparagus. Refill the saucepan with water and bring it to a boil. Add the asparagus and cook until tender but still firm, approximately 3 minutes. Remove from the boiling water and set in the ice water with the leeks and carrots.

5. When the artichokes are cooked, remove all the leaves and "chokes" from the hearts. Place the hearts in a food processor and blend until smooth.

6. Pour 1/3 cup water into a small saucepan. Stir in the gelatin and let rest for 1 minute, then stir over low heat until dissolved, aproximately 3 minutes. Add to the artichoke purée. Add the chopped tarragon and season with salt and pepper to taste.

Continued on next page

26

Artichoke and Asparagus Terrine with Beet Vinaigrette

Continued

7. Line the sides of a 10-inch or 12-inch loaf pan with parchment paper. Then, using the reserved single leaves of the leek, line the inside of the pan, overlapping the edges by 2 inches on the sides.

8. To create the terrine, layer ingredients as follows: artichoke purée, sliced carrots, puree, whole leeks, purée, whole asparagus, purée. Gently press the vegetables into purée as you layer them. Continue layering until the loaf pan is full, ending with a layer of purée.

9. Fold the ends of the leek leaves over the top of the mold to cover the purée layers. Wrap in plastic and chill at least 12 hours. This can be made up to three days ahead.

10. To serve, unmold the terrine and slice into 1-inch servings. It is easier to slice if you use an electric knife. Drizzle Beet Vinaigrette decoratively on each plate.

Serving Size: 10

Beet Vinaigrette

1/2 POUND BEETS, PEELED AND DICED

1/4 CUP RED WINE VINEGAR

1/2 CUP EXTRA VIRGIN OLIVE OIL

SALT AND PEPPER

1. Preheat the oven to 350 degrees.

2. Wrap the diced beet in aluminum foil and roast for 45 minutes. Let cool.

3. Transfer the beet to a blender and add the vinegar. With the motor running, slowly add the olive oil and blend until mixed.

4. Season with salt and pepper to taste, then chill until ready to serve.

Serving Size: 10

Spiced Mustard Sauce

¹/₄ CUP PREPARED CHICKEN STOCK

2 TEASPOONS DIJON MUSTARD

1 TEASPOON WASABI PASTE,
OR MORE TO TASTE

¹/₂ TEASPOON DRY MUSTARD

2 TEASPOONS SOY SAUCE

¹/₃ CUP PEANUT OIL

PINCH OF CAYENNE PEPPER

SALT AND PEPPER

1. In a mixing bowl, whisk together chicken stock, Dijon mustard, wasabi paste, dry mustard, and soy sauce.

2. Transfer to a blender and while the motor is running, slowly add the oil. Season with cayenne, salt and pepper to taste. If the sauce is too thick, blend in more chicken stock.

3. Chill until ready to serve.

Serving Size: 6

Dungeness Crab and Crispy Noodle Galette with Spiced Mustard Sauce

A Venice original – These bundles of fried noodles with spiced crab in the center look like free-form sculpture, edible art! If Dungeness Crab is not available, substitute Blue Crab. Don't let the looseness of the noodle bundles worry you. When they are cooked they will hold together nicely.

8 CUPS WATER

12 OUNCES ANGEL HAIR PASTA

1 TABLESPOON PEANUT OIL

2 WHOLE DUNGENESS CRABS, COOKED,
OR 1 POUND FLAKED CRABMEAT

1 RED BELL PEPPER, FINELY DICED

1 TABLESPOON CHOPPED CELERY

1 TABLESPOON GRATED FRESH GINGER

1 TEASPOON CHOPPED GREEN ONION,
WHITE PART ONLY

2 SHALLOTS, CHOPPED

PEANUT OIL FOR SAUTÉING

SPICED MUSTARD SAUCE
(SEE RECIPE ON FACING PAGE)

WHOLE CHIVES

1. In a large pot, bring water to a boil. Add the pasta and boil for 3 minutes. Strain. Toss with 1 tablespoon oil and cool slightly. Spread the cooked noodles out on a cookie sheet and refrigerate until completely cold so they don't stick together. When cold, the pasta may be stored in a covered dish or a baggie until ready to use. (This may be done up to one day ahead.)

2. Remove the crabmeat from the shell and flake.

3. Combine red and green peppers, celery, ginger, green onion, and shallots with the crabmeat and mix well.

4. Divide both the pasta and the crab mixture into six equal portions. Holding a portion of pasta in your hand, top with the crab mixture and bring the pasta up around it so that the crab mixture is covered. The pasta will be loose, so the finished galette will be somewhat free-form. For easier handling, set each bundle on a square of wax paper or parchment paper until all bundles are prepared.

5. Heat enough peanut oil to cover bottom of a sauté pan over medium heat. When oil is very hot, add the galettes and cook for about 4 minutes per side, or until golden brown. Depending on the size of your pan, you may need to do this in batches, adding more oil if necessary.

6. Serve with Spiced Mustard Sauce and garnish with whole chives.

Serving Size: 6

The Honorable Matt Fong, California State Treasurer, and Paula Fong – "Party Politics"
CRAB CAKES WITH BELUGA CAVIAR
photographed by Pablo Aguilar

These tasty cakes were on the first menu at 72. We now offer them often on the "Specials"
menu and as an hors d'oeuvre at parties. To simplify the recipe, you may use green bell
pepper only, in place of the yellow and red bell peppers. In either case, the peppers should
be chopped by hand, not with a food processor, or they will become mushy.

Crab Cakes with Beluga Caviar

1 POUND FLAKED CRABMEAT

2 TABLESPOONS MINCED GREEN BELL PEPPER

2 TABLESPOONS MINCED RED BELL PEPPER

2 TABLESPOONS MINCED YELLOW BELL PEPPER

2 TABLESPOONS MINCED YELLOW ONION

2 TABLESPOONS MINCED GREEN ONION

2 TABLESPOONS MINCED CELERY

3 TABLESPOONS MELTED BUTTER

1 TEASPOON DIJON MUSTARD

$1/4$ TEASPOON SALT

$1/8$ TABLESPOON GROUND WHITE PEPPER

$1/8$ TEASPOON CAYENNE PEPPER

$1/8$ TEASPOON NUTMEG

$1/8$ TEASPOON PAPRIKA

2 TEASPOONS LEMON JUICE

1 EGG, BEATEN

$1/3$ CUP WHIPPING CREAM

$1/2$ CUP PREPARED BREADCRUMBS

$1/2$ CUP SOUR CREAM

1 TABLESPOON MINCED SHALLOT

SALT AND PEPPER

4 OUNCES BELUGA CAVIAR

1. Pick over the crabmeat to remove any shells, then set aside.

2. Sauté the minced green, red, and yellow peppers with the yellow and green onion and celery in 1 tablespoon of the melted butter, until the vegetables are slightly limp, about 5 minutes. Remove from heat and let cool completely.

3. In a medium bowl, mix together the mustard, salt, pepper, cayenne, nutmeg, paprika, 1 teaspoon of the lemon juice, the beaten egg, and the whipping cream.

4. Add the crabmeat, the cooked vegetables, and bread-crumbs. Mix well.

5. In a separate bowl, mix together the sour cream, shallot and the remaining 1 teaspoon of lemon juice. Season with salt and pepper to taste. Set aside.

6. Divide the crab mixture into 16 patties.

7. Heat 2 tablespoons of the melted butter in a sauté pan, and cook the patties until golden brown, about 3 minutes on each side. Remove from the pan and pat dry with a paper towel. Keep warm until ready to serve.

8. To serve, place two crab cakes on each plate and top with a dollop of the sour cream mixture. Top with $1/2$-ounce of caviar.

Serving Size: 8

Seymour Cassel, Actor - "Up in Smoke"
CHICKEN SATAY
photographed by Danny Duchovny

You can use the reserved marinade as a dipping sauce, but do not use the marinade in
which the chicken has been sitting, as it will contain raw chicken juices. Soak skewers in
water overnight before using to prevent the wood from burning on the grill.

Chicken Satay with
Peanut Dipping Sauce

2 WHOLE CHICKEN BREASTS,
BONED AND SKINNED

¹/₄ CUP CANNED COCONUT MILK

¹/₄ CUP SMOOTH PEANUT BUTTER

1 TABLESPOON FRESH LIME JUICE

2¹/₄ TEASPOONS BROWN SUGAR, PACKED

³/₄ TEASPOON CHOPPED FRESH GINGER

³/₄ TEASPOON CHOPPED GREEN ONION

³/₄ TEASPOON FINELY DICED JALAPEÑO

¹/₄ TEASPOON TAHINI, OR SESAME OIL
(OPTIONAL)

DASH OF CRUSHED RED PEPPER

DASH OF TURMERIC

DASH OF GROUND CLOVES

4 TEASPOONS PEANUT OIL

24 WOODEN SKEWERS

1. Cut the chicken breasts lengthwise into strips that are about ¹/4-inch wide and 2 to 3 inches long. Set aside.

2. In a medium bowl, whisk together the coconut milk, peanut butter, and lime juice.

3. Stir in the brown sugar, ginger, green onion, jalapeño, tahini, crushed red pepper, turmeric, and cloves.

4. Slowly whisk in the oil, beating until completely blended.

5. Skewer the chicken by threading each piece in an S-shape onto a skewer. Place skewers in a shallow pan and baste with the marinade, reserving some marinade for dipping. Cover and chill for 2 hours.

6. Heat the grill or barbecue and cook skewered chicken over medium-high heat until it is no longer pink, about 3 minutes on each side.

Serving Size: 24 skewers

Salads

72

Katherine Bonner, "The Little Mermaid"......................36

12 Crayfish Salad Wrapped in Smoked Salmon
with Mango Vinaigrette..37

Connie Linn, "In Living Color"..38

13 Maine Lobster Napoleon
with Mango Vinaigrette..39

14 Warm Pear and Roquefort Torte
with Salad Greens and Red Wine Vinaigrette............40

15 Grilled Seafood and Vegetable Salad
with Lemon Vinaigrette..43

*Nancy Kay and E.F. Kitchen
with Boris and Igor, "Photo Op"*...44

16 Calamari Salad...45

Aleiza and Lysandra, "Chopstix".......................................46

17 Chinese Chicken Salad..47

Peter Alexander, "Lunch in the Abstract".........................48

18 Grilled Portabello Mushrooms and a Small
Mesclun with Red Bell Pepper Vinaigrette 49

David Baerwald, "After Hours"...50

19 Fall Fruit Salad...51

Katherine Bonner, Illustrator/Photographer - "The Little Mermaid"
CRAYFISH SALAD WRAPPED IN SMOKED SALMON WITH MANGO VINAIGRETTE
photographed by Christine Caldwell

A dazzling first course or luncheon entrée. If you are able to find fresh crayfish and cook them yourself, you will taste the difference, because freezing causes the flesh of the crayfish to become slightly watery.

Crayfish Salad Wrapped in Smoked Salmon with Mango Vinaigrette

1 BUNCH TARRAGON

1 ONION, SLICED

1 CARROT, SLICED

1 CELERY STALK, SLICED

1 CUP WHITE WINE

1 SPRIG THYME

1 BAY LEAF

3 POUNDS FRESH CRAYFISH, ABOUT 36 TO 40, OR FROZEN

1 CARROT, FINELY DICED

1 CELERY STALK, FINELY DICED

1/4 POUND HARICOTS VERTS (OR GREEN BEANS), FINELY DICED

1/4 POUND YELLOW WAX BEANS, FINELY DICED

MANGO VINAIGRETTE (SEE RECIPE ON PAGE 39)

1/4 POUND SMOKED SALMON, CUT INTO 4 VERY THIN SLICES

1. To cook live crayfish, bring 3 quarts of water to a boil. Prepare a court bouillon by adding the tarragon, onion, sliced carrot, sliced celery, white wine, thyme, and bay leaf to the water. Boil for five minutes. Add the crayfish and continue to boil for 4 minutes. Remove the crayfish from their shells and shred the tail meat into small pieces. Reserve the shells to decorate plates.

2. In a saucepan of boiling salted water, cook the diced carrot until tender, about 2 to 3 minutes. Repeat with the celery, haricots verts, and wax beans, cooking each vegetable separately.

3. Prepare the Mango Vinaigrette and set aside until ready to use.

4. Combine three-quarters of each vegetable, the crayfish, and the Mango Vinaigrette and mix well. If you like, reserve a little Mango Vinaigrette to decorate the serving dish.

5. Place a slice of smoked salmon on a piece of plastic wrap. Place one-quarter of the crayfish mixture in the center of the salmon. Bunch up the sides of the plastic and twist the top closed. Carefully remove the plastic and the place bundle, seam side, down on a serving plate. Chill until ready to serve.

6. Garnish salmon bundles with the remaining vegetables and crayfish. Serve cold, using the reserved shells as decoration.

Serving Size: 4

Connie Linn, Patron – "In Living Color"
LOBSTER NAPOLEON WITH MANGO VINAIGRETTE
photographed by Danny Duchovny

Serving lobster makes any meal a celebration. This dish is simple to prepare, and you can dress it up by decorating the serving dish with the lobster head, legs and tail.

Maine Lobster Napoleon with Mango Vinaigrette

2 1-POUND MAINE LOBSTERS, ABOUT
³/₄ CUP COOKED LOBSTER MEAT

4 CUPS MIXED GREENS

2 ROMA TOMATOES, SEEDED AND DICED

4 LARGE MUSHROOMS, SLICED

MANGO VINAIGRETTE

1 AVOCADO, PEELED AND SLICED THIN

1 MANGO, PEELED AND SLICED THIN

1 Remove the meat from the lobster shell and slice into medallions. Reserve the claws to decorate the serving dish. Chill.

2 Toss the greens, tomato, and mushrooms with the Mango Vinaigrette, reserving some to finish the dish.

3 In a small serving bowl, spread alternate layers of the greens mixture, mango, avocado, and lobster, packing down until the bowl is filled.

4 Invert the bowl onto a plate to unmold.

5 Sprinkle with more Mango Vinaigrette or use a squeeze bottle to make a design.

Serving Size: 4

Mango Vinaigrette

1 RIPE MANGO, PEELED AND DICED

¹/₂ CUP SHERRY VINEGAR

1 TEASPOON DIJON MUSTARD

¹/₂ CUP PEANUT OIL

SALT AND PEPPER

CAYENNE PEPPER

1 Place the mango, vinegar, and mustard in a blender. With the motor running, slowly add the peanut oil and blend on medium speed for 1 minute.

2 Season with salt and pepper and cayenne pepper to taste. Chill until ready to serve.

Serving Size: 6

*Very simple, very French. If you make the tarts smaller, they can be served as hors d'oeuvres.
The ripeness of the pear is crucial to the flavor of the tart; Stilton, gorgonzola or Danish
blue cheese may be substituted for the Roquefort if you prefer.*

Warm Pear and Roquefort Torte with Salad Greens and Red Wine Vinaigrette

FOR THE TORTES:

1 BOX FROZEN PUFF PASTRY SHEETS

1 EGG YOLK PLUS 1 TEASPOON WATER

1 RIPE ANJOU PEAR

1 CUP SUGAR

2 CUPS WATER

8 OUNCES ROQUEFORT CHEESE, CRUMBLED

FOR THE SALAD:

2 CUPS MIXED SALAD GREENS

1/2 TEASPOON CHOPPED TARRAGON

1/2 TEASPOON CHOPPED CHIVES

1/2 TEASPOON CHOPPED ITALIAN PARSLEY

1/2 TEASPOON CHOPPED CHERVIL

RED WINE VINAIGRETTE (ON FACING PAGE)

3 TABLESPOONS CHOPPED WALNUTS

1. To prepare the puff pastry: Preheat oven to 375 degrees. Using a 4-inch saucer as a guide, cut the frozen sheets into four 4-inch circles. Beat the egg yolk with 1 teaspoon of the water. Place puff pastry circles on lightly greased cookie sheet and brush with egg yolk and water mixture so the dough will glaze. Bake at 375 degrees for 15 to 18 minutes or until lightly browned. Be sure the dough is cooked through and not mushy inside. Remove from the oven and set aside.

2. To poach the pear: Peel and core the pear and cut in half. Combine the sugar and 2 cups of water in a saucepan. Bring to a boil. Add the pear and cook on high until it can be easily pierced with a fork, about 3 to 4 minutes. Remove the pear from the water and cool. Slice each half lengthwise into 4 pieces

3. Slice the puff pastry circles in half horizontally, making a top and a bottom. It is easiest to do this with an electric knife, but it can also be done with a serrated knife, cutting slowly and carefully. On four pastry halves, place 2 ounces of Roquefort; place two slices of pear on the others. (If you prefer to use less cheese, you may reduce the amount accordingly.)

4. Place the puff pastry circles back on the cookie sheet and bake in at 375 degrees until the cheese is melted, about 5 minutes.

Continued on next page

Warm Pear and Roquefort Torte with Salad Greens and Red Wine Vinaigrette

Continued

5   Remove the pastry from the oven and put the cheese half of the pastry on top of the pear half.

6   Mix together the salad greens and herbs and toss with Red Wine Vinaigrette.

7   To serve, put a torte on the dish and surround it with dressed greens. Sprinkle chopped walnuts on top.

Serving Size: 4

Red Wine Vinaigrette

1 TABLESPOON DIJON MUSTARD

¹/₄ CUP RED WINE VINEGAR

³/₄ CUP PECAN OIL OR PEANUT OIL

SALT AND PEPPER

1   Combine Dijon mustard, vinegar, oil, and salt and pepper to taste in a blender.

2   Blend on high until the oil is fully incorporated.

3   Chill. Serve with mixed greens.

Serving Size: 6

Lemon Vinaigrette

¹/₄ CUP FRESH LEMON JUICE

¹/₂ TEASPOON WHOLE-GRAIN MUSTARD

¹/₄ CUP OLIVE OIL

¹/₄ CUP EXTRA VIRGIN OLIVE OIL

SALT AND PEPPER

1 Combine the lemon juice and mustard in a blender.

2 With the motor running, slowly add both oils, blending until smooth.

3 Season to taste with salt and pepper. Chill until ready to use.

Serving Size: 6

Grilled Seafood and Vegetable Salad with Lemon Vinaigrette

BAMBOO SKEWERS, SOAKED IN
WATER OVERNIGHT

3/4 POUND SEA BASS, DICED INTO
1/2-INCH CUBES

1/2 POUND ROCK SHRIMP, PEELED
AND DEVEINED

1/2 POUND BAY SCALLOPS

2 TABLESPOONS EXTRA VIRGIN OLIVE OIL

SALT AND PEPPER

2 CARROTS, CUT LENGTHWISE INTO
1/4-INCH SLICES

1 SMALL EGGPLANT, UNPEELED,
SLICED LENGTHWISE

2 ZUCCHINI, UNPEELED,
SLICED LENGTHWISE

6 CUPS MIXED GREENS

LEMON VINAIGRETTE
(SEE RECIPE ON FACING PAGE)

1 Heat the barbecue grill.

2 Divide the sea bass, shrimp, and scallops into six equal portions and skewer each portion. Brush with olive oil and season with salt and pepper to taste.

3 Skewer the carrots, eggplant, and zucchini slices. Lightly brush with olive oil and season with salt and pepper to taste.

4 Grill the fish and vegetables over medium heat until done, about 2 minutes on each side.

5 Toss the mixed greens with the Lemon Vinaigrette. Arrange the vegetables and skewered fish on each plate and serve immediately.

Serving Size: 6

Nancy Kay, Artist, and E.F. Kitchen, Photographer, with Boris and Igor - "Photo Op"
GRILLED SEAFOOD AND VEGETABLE SALAD WITH LEMON VINAIGRETTE
photographed by E.F. Kitchen

For calamari lovers, this is a light alternative to the fried version. You will probably find the calamari in frozen form. Fortunately, neither the flavor nor the texture is altered by freezing. Thaw before using. You may use whole calamari or calamari steak for this recipe — we prefer the whole calamari.

Calamari Salad

2 ¹/₂ POUNDS CALAMARI, CLEANED

¹/₄ CUP EXTRA VIRGIN OLIVE OIL

1 TABLESPOON LEMON JUICE

1¹/₂ TEASPOONS CHOPPED PARSLEY

1¹/₂ TEASPOONS CRUSHED RED PEPPER

1¹/₂ TEASPOONS MINCED GARLIC

³/₄ TABLESPOON PEPPER

¹/₂ CUP BABY ARTICHOKE HEARTS PACKED IN WATER, SLICED

2 TABLESPOONS CAPERS

SALT AND PEPPER

1 Fill an 8-cup stockpot with water and bring to a boil. Add the calamari. Return to a boil and cook on high, uncovered, for 3 minutes.

2 Strain and chill the calamari. If you are using whole calamari, slice it into rings approximately ¹/4-inch thick. If you are using calamari steak, julienne into ¹/4-inch strips.

3 In a mixing bowl, combine the olive oil. lemon juice, parsley, crushed red pepper, garlic, and pepper, and stir until well blended. Add the baby artichoke hearts, capers, and calamari rings. Toss and season with salt and pepper to taste.

Serving Size: 6

Aleiza and Lysandra - "Chopstix"
CHINESE CHICKEN SALAD
photographed by Ronald Cadiz

This superb recipe was created by Luis Hernandez, our lunch cook. Be sure to note that only the skin of the cucumber is used and not its watery flesh, thus adding only the flavor and texture of the vegetable. We get raves for this salad. Bravo, Luis!

Chinese Chicken Salad

3 WHOLE GRILLED CHICKEN BREASTS, SKINNED

4 CUPS ROMAINE LETTUCE

1 CARROT

1 CELERY STALK

1 CUCUMBER, SKIN ONLY

1 RED BELL PEPPER

$1/2$ CUP PEANUT OIL

$1/2$ CUP COOKED ANGEL HAIR PASTA

$1/2$ CUP WONTON SKINS, CUT INTO $1/4$-INCH STRIPS

JAPANESE VINAIGRETTE (SEE RECIPE ON PAGE 16)

1 PACKAGE DAIKON SPROUTS

1   Dice the cooked chicken into $1/2$-inch cubes. Chill.

2   Shred the romaine lettuce and cut the carrot, celery, cucumber skin, and red bell pepper into julienne strips.

3   Heat the oil in a small sauté pan. Add the angel hair pasta and fry over high heat until golden brown and crisp. Remove from the oil with a slotted spoon and drain on paper towels.

4   Add the wonton skins to the remaining hot oil. Fry until golden brown and crisp. Remove from the oil with a slotted spoon and drain on paper towels.

5   Combine diced chicken, romaine, julienned vegetables, angel hair pasta, and wonton skins, and toss with Japanese Vinaigrette. To serve, top with daikon sprouts.

Serving Size: 6

Peter Alexander, Artist – "Lunch in the Abstract"
AT THE OYSTER BAR
photographed by Gillian Lefcowitz

Mushrooms are very absorbent. Since they will become mushy if you marinate them for any length of time, it's best to brush the marinade onto the mushroom cap just prior to grilling. 'Mesclun' is a French word that refers to a mixture of small, wild-tasting leaves and shoots. We use it here to suggest a salad of mixed greens.

Grilled Portobello Mushrooms and a Small Mesclun with Red Pepper Vinaigrette

FOR THE VINAIGRETTE:

1 RED BELL PEPPER

$1/2$ TEASPOON DIJON MUSTARD

1 TEASPOON SHERRY VINEGAR

1 TABLESPOON PEANUT OIL

FOR THE MUSHROOMS:

2 TEASPOONS BALSAMIC VINEGAR

2 TABLESPOONS EXTRA VIRGIN OLIVE OIL

2 TEASPOONS CHOPPED GARLIC

4 PORTOBELLO MUSHROOMS, ABOUT 6 INCHES IN DIAMETER

FOR THE MESCLUN:

3 CUPS MIXED BABY GREENS

2 ROMA TOMATOES, PREFERABLY YELLOW, HALVED AND HOLLOWED OUT

2 TEASPOONS CHOPPED CHIVES

1. For the Red Pepper Vinaigrette: Prepare the grill or barbecue. Char the red pepper over high heat until blackened. Put the charred pepper in a brown bag or cover tightly with a dish towel for a few minutes to steam. This will loosen the charred skin. Remove the skin and seeds. Transfer to a blender.

2. Add the Dijon mustard, sherry vinegar, and peanut oil to the blender. Purée and season to taste. Chill dressing until ready to use.

3. Combine the balsamic vinegar, olive oil, and chopped garlic, and baste the mushrooms with the mixture.

4. Grill the mushrooms over medium-high heat for 3 minutes on each side, basting again when the mushrooms are turned.

5. To serve, slice the mushrooms and drizzle with Red Pepper Vinaigrette. Garnish with salad greens tossed with Red Pepper Vinaigrette and bundled into the hollowed-out Roma tomatoes. Top with chives.

Serving Size: 4

David Baerwald, Musician - "After Hours"
FALL FRUIT SALAD
photographed by Gillian Lefcowitz

This salad lives up to its name — both the persimmon and the pomegranate are only

Fall Fruit Salad

available in the fall. Of course you can substitute other fruits for these two. Just be sure
whatever variety you buy is perfectly ripe, has a fruity aroma, and gives a little to the
touch when you press on the flesh.

4 CUPS FRISÉE LEAVES
(CURLY ENDIVE)

3 TABLESPOONS LIME JUICE

3 TABLESPOONS RICE VINEGAR

2 TABLESPOONS HONEY

SALT

2 PERSIMMONS, PEELED AND SLICED

1 BARTLETT PEAR, PEELED,
CORED AND SLICED

2 TABLESPOONS PINE NUTS

2 GRAPEFRUITS, PEELED AND
SECTIONED WITH MEMBRANES REMOVED

1 POMEGRANATE, SEEDS ONLY

1 Wash the frisée leaves and pat dry. Chill.

2 To make the dressing: Combine lime juice, rice vinegar and honey. Season with salt if desired. Chill.

3 Shred the frisée and place in a mixing bowl with persimmon slices, pear slices, and pine nuts. Toss with dressing.

4 To assemble: Place grapefruit segments around each serving plate and put mixed salad in the center. Garnish with pomegranate seeds.

Serving Size: 6

Soups

72

Mary Steenburgen and Ted Danson,
"Soup du Jour" 54

20 Spicy Corn Chowder 55

21 Seafood Gumbo with Rock Shrimp 56

22 Lobster Bisque 57

23 Mushroom Bisque 58

24 Black Bean Soup 59

Sharon Jacobucci and Leslie Bisno,
"Meal Ticket" 60

25 Vegetable Split Pea Soup 61

Wendy Al and Billy Al Bengston,
"The First Time I Ever Liked Gazpacho" 62

26 Gazpacho 63

27 Sweet Potato Clam Chowder 64

28 Cream of Parsnip Soup with Ginger 65

Ted Danson and Mary Steenburgen, Actors - "Soup du Jour"
SPICY CORN CHOWDER
photographed by Gillian Lefcowitz

A summer favorite! Using corn husks to flavor the base of the soup enriches the taste. Buy locally grown corn if possible, and store it in the refrigerator, unhusked and wrapped in a damp towel until ready to use.

Spicy Corn Chowder

6 FRESH COBS OF CORN, SILKS REMOVED
AND HUSKS RESERVED

2 QUARTS WATER

3 TABLESPOONS PEANUT OIL

1 RED BELL PEPPER, FINELY DICED

3/4 CUP DICED ONION

1/4 CUP DICED CELERY

3/4 TEASPOON FRESH THYME

3/4 TEASPOON FRESH PARSLEY

3/4 TEASPOON PEPPER

1/2 TEASPOON CAYENNE PEPPER

3/4 TEASPOON SALT

PAPRIKA

1   Cut the corn from the cob and reserve. Reserve 2 of the husks and cobs, and discard the others.

2   In a stockpot, boil the reserved corn cobs and husks in two quarts of water for 15 minutes. Strain and reserve liquid. Discard the husks and cobs

3   In the same stockpot, heat the peanut oil and sauté the red bell pepper, onion, and celery until tender, about 6 minutes.

4   Add the reserved corn. Stir in the thyme, parsley, pepper, and cayenne pepper.

5   Add the reserved corn husk liquid and bring to a boil. Season with salt and paprika.

Serving Size: 6

The addition of the gumbo filé gives this soup an authentic Louisiana flavor. Be sure not to cook the soup after the filé has been added, or the broth will become ropy. The pork sausage will probably come packaged in bulk. If possible, try to find a brand that has no added herbs or seasonings.

Seafood Gumbo with Rock Shrimp

1 BAY LEAF

2 CLOVES

3 WHOLE ALLSPICE

1/4 CUP PEANUT OIL

1/2 CUP ALL-PURPOSE FLOUR

1/2 CUP CHOPPED ONION

1 RED BELL PEPPER, CHOPPED

1 GREEN BELL PEPPER, CHOPPED

1/3 CUP CHOPPED GREEN ONION

2 TEASPOONS CHOPPED PARSLEY

1/2 CUP CHOPPED TOMATOES

1 1/4 PINTS FISH STOCK

6 OUNCES LEAN GROUND PORK SAUSAGE

12 JUMBO SHRIMP,
SHELLED AND DEVEINED

1 TEASPOON OLIVE OIL

SALT AND PEPPER

1 TEASPOON GUMBO FILÉ

1. Tie the bay leaf, clove, and allspice in a piece of cheesecloth to make a spice bundle.

2. In a stockpot, make a brown roux by cooking the peanut oil and the flour until medium brown, about 10 minutes, whisking constantly so it does not burn.

3. Add the onion, red bell pepper, green bell pepper, green onion, parsley, and tomato, and sauté for 10 minutes.

4. Stir in the fish stock, sausage, and the spice bundle and simmer, covered, for 35 minutes.

5. Meanwhile, sauté the peeled shrimp in olive oil for 2 minutes on each side, or until cooked through and no longer opaque.

6. When the soup is fully cooked, remove cheesecloth bundle of spices. Season with salt and pepper to taste. Add the gumbo filé.

7. Ladle the gumbo into bowls and use shrimp to garnish.

Serving Size: 6

A rich but impressive first course. The taste of the lobster is enhanced by simmering the shells in fish stock for the broth. Be sure to strain well before serving to remove all the small pieces! If you don't have cream of rice cereal you can substitute 1 tablespoon of arrowroot dissolved in 2 teaspoons of water, then just whisk the dissolved arrowroot into the bisque after straining.

4 QUARTS WATER

2 MAINE LOBSTERS, PREFERABLY LIVE

1 1/2 TABLESPOONS BUTTER

1 CELERY STALK, MINCED

1 MEDIUM ONION, MINCED

1 GARLIC CLOVE, MINCED

2 TEASPOONS PAPRIKA

1 1/2 TEASPOONS TOMATO PASTE

1 SPRIG FRESH TARRAGON

2 TABLESPOONS SHERRY

4 CUPS FISH STOCK

3 TABLESPOONS CREAM OF RICE CEREAL

1 CUP WHIPPING CREAM

SALT AND PEPPER

1 OUNCE BRANDY

1 BAGUETTE FRENCH BREAD

OLIVE OIL

2 GARLIC CLOVES

GRATED PARMESAN CHEESE

1. Bring 4 quarts of water to a boil. Place lobsters in the water and cook for 3 minutes. Remove and cool slightly.

2. Crack each lobster carcass to remove the meat from the tail and claws, and aside.

3. Put the lobster shells and body in a sturdy plastic bag and crush using a mallet or a hammer.

4. Melt the butter in a large stockpot. Add the shells, celery, and onion, and sauté over medium heat for 3 minutes, or until the onion is translucent.

5. Add the garlic, paprika, tomato paste, and tarragon. Stir in the sherry and cook for an additional 2 minutes over medium heat.

6. Add the fish stock and bring to a boil over high heat. Reduce to low heat and simmer, uncovered, for 25 minutes. Strain the broth and return to heat.

7. While broth is simmering make the croutons: Slice the baguette into 1/2-inch-square pieces. Sprinkle with oil, and toast on a cookie sheet in a 400-degree oven, until golden.

8. Add the cream of rice to the broth. Bring to a boil and cook for 1 minute, stirring.

9. Put the broth in a blender and purée in batches until smooth. While the motor is running, add the cream. Adjust seasonings with salt and pepper to taste.

10. Return to pot and stir in the lobster meat and the brandy. Bring to a simmer and ladle into bowls.

11. Cut garlic cloves in half and rub onto the toasted croutons. Place croutons on top of the bisque and sprinkle with Paramesan cheese.

Serving Size: 6

Mushroom Bisque

2 TABLESPOONS BUTTER

1/2 CUP CHOPPED ONION

1/4 CUP CHOPPED LEEK,
WHITE PART ONLY

1 1/2 POUNDS CHOPPED
BUTTON MUSHROOMS

1/4 BUNCH THYME, MINCED

1/4 BUNCH TARRAGON, MINCED

1 BAY LEAF

1/2 TEASPOON MINCED GARLIC

5 CUPS CHICKEN STOCK

SALT AND PEPPER

1 Melt the butter in a stockpot. Add the onion, leek, mushrooms, thyme, tarragon, and bay leaf. Sauté over medium heat, stirring constantly, until onions are translucent, about 7 minutes.

2 Add garlic and sauté for 2 more minutes.

3 Add chicken stock and bring to a boil. Reduce heat to simmer, cover, and cook for 10 minutes.

4 Remove bay leaf and purée. Season with salt and pepper to taste.

Serving Size: 6

Black Bean Soup

1 ¹/₂ CUPS BLACK BEANS

1 TABLESPOON EXTRA VIRGIN OLIVE OIL

¹/₃ CUP DICED ONION

1 CELERY STALK, DICED

¹/₄ CUP DICED CARROT

¹/₃ RED BELL PEPPER, DICED

¹/₃ GREEN BELL PEPPER, DICED

2 TEASPOONS FRESH THYME, MINCED

1 TEASPOON JALAPEÑO,
SEEDED AND DICED

1 GARLIC CLOVE, MINCED

1 ROMA TOMATO, PEELED, SEEDED,
AND DICED

SALT AND PEPPER

1. Soak black beans in 10 cups of water to cover for 24 hours.

2. Heat olive oil in a stockpot. Add the onion, celery, carrot, red bell pepper, green bell pepper, thyme, and jalapeño. Sauté for 5 to 7 minutes or until the vegetables are tender and the onions translucent.

3. Add the garlic and tomato and sauté for 3 more minutes.

4. Strain the black beans, reserving the soaking water. Add the beans to the stockpot and measure the soaking water, adding enough plain water to make 6 ¹/₂ cups. Add the water to the stock pot and bring to a boil.

5. Cover, and simmer over low heat for 35 to 45 minutes, or until the black beans are tender. You may need to add additional water if you find the soup is too thick.

6. Purée and season with salt and pepper to taste.

Serving Size: 6

Sharon Jacobucci, Metermaid and Leslie Bisno, Waiter - "Meal Ticket"
VEGETABLE SPLIT PEA SOUP
photographed by Danny Duchovny

Vegetable Split Pea Soup

3/4 CUP DRY SPLIT PEAS

6 CUPS WATER

2 TEASPOONS OLIVE OIL

1/2 CUP DICED CARROT

1/2 CUP DICED TURNIP

1/2 CUP DICED ZUCCHINI

1/2 CUP DICED CELERY

1/2 CUP DICED LEEK

1/2 CUP DICED ONION

1/2 CUP DICED GREEN BELL PEPPER

1 TEASPOON FINELY CHOPPED GARLIC

1 SPRIG FRESH THYME

BAY LEAF

PARSLEY STEMS

SALT AND PEPPER

1. In a stockpot, bring the split peas and the water to a boil. Reduce heat and simmer until soft, about 25 to 30 minutes. Set both peas and water aside.

2. In another stockpot, heat the olive oil, and add the carrot, turnip, zucchini, celery, leek, onion, and green bell pepper. Sauté for 7 minutes over medium heat, or until the onion is translucent.

3. Add the garlic and sauté for 3 more minutes.

4. Tie the sprig of thyme, the bay leaf, and parsley stems together with a string to form a bouquet garni.

5. Add the split peas. Measure the water the peas were cooked in and added additional water to make 6 1/2 cups. Add the water and the bouquet garni to the vegetables and simmer, covered, for 15 minutes.

6. Adjust seasoning with salt and pepper to taste. Discard the bouquet garni, and serve hot.

Serving Size: 6

Billy Al Bengston, Owner/Director of Billy's Studio, and Wendy Al – "The First Time I Ever Liked Gazpacho"
GAZPACHO
photographed by Michael Cullen

The fresher and crisper the vegetables you use in this healthy classic, the better the taste.

Beware — some root vegetables, such as onions, develop a stronger flavor if they are old, and

Gazpacho

might overpower the more delicate flavors of the tomato, cucumber, and green bell pepper.

If you prefer a chunkier soup, purée only half of the vegetables.

8 ROMA TOMATOES, PEELED, SEEDED, AND DICED

1 CUCUMBER, PEELED, SEEDED, AND DICED

1 ONION, DICED

1 GREEN BELL PEPPER, DICED

1 JALAPEÑO, DICED

4 GARLIC CLOVES, DICED

1 QUART TOMATO JUICE

1/2 CUP RED WINE VINEGAR

1/2 CUP EXTRA VIRGIN OLIVE OIL

1 TEASPOON CAYENNE PEPPER

1 TEASPOON SALT

1 TEASPOON PEPPER

1 Place all the ingredients in a covered container to marinate. Chill for at least 24 hours.

2 Purée in batches, season to taste, and chill until ready to serve.

Serving Size: 8

Sweet Potato Clam Chowder

36 LITTLENECK CLAMS

4 CUPS WATER

3 OUNCES LEAN BACON, DICED

2 TABLESPOONS BUTTER

1 1/2 CUPS FINELY CHOPPED ONION

3/4 CUP LIGHT CREAM

2 CUPS MILK

2 MEDIUM SWEET POTATOES,
PEELED AND FINELY DICED

1 TEASPOON FRESH THYME

SALT AND PEPPER

1. Scrub the clams and check to make sure none are open.

2. Put 2 cups of the water and the clams in an 8-cup stockpot and bring to a boil. Cook, uncovered, over high heat until clams open, about 5 minutes. Strain and reserve the liquid. Discard any clams that do not open.

3. Remove the meat from the clams and dice. Do not use the rubber-like attachment called the foot, which holds the meat to the clam shell.

4. Place the remaining 2 cups of water in the stockpot and add the diced bacon. Blanch by boiling, uncovered, for 2 minutes, skimming the foam from the top as it forms. Strain, and pour off the liquid, reserving bacon. Rinse out the pot.

5. Return the bacon to the stockpot and fry until crisp.

6. Remove the bacon and add the butter and onion to the grease. Cook over medium heat until translucent, about 5 minutes.

7. Add the reserved clam liquid and the cream. Bring to a boil. Add the milk and sweet potato and simmer for 10 minutes. Stir in the bacon, clams, and thyme and cook for an additional 3 minutes. Season with salt and pepper to taste. Serve hot.

Serving Size: 6

Cream of Parsnip Soup with Ginger

2 TABLESPOONS BUTTER

1 MEDIUM ONION, DICED

1 CELERY STALK, DICED

4 PARSNIPS, SLICED

2 TEASPOONS MINCED FRESH GINGER

6 CUPS VEGETABLE STOCK OR WATER

1 TEASPOON SALT

1 1/2 CUPS WHIPPING CREAM

1/2 TEASPOON TURMERIC

SALT AND PEPPER

1. Melt the butter in stockpot. Add onion, celery, parsnip, and ginger. Sauté for 7 minutes over medium heat, stirring occasionally, until the vegetables are translucent, but not browned.

2. Add the vegetable stock or water, and bring to a boil. Reduce to low heat and simmer, covered, for 10 minutes.

3. Add the salt, cream, and turmeric. Bring soup back to a boil, then remove from heat immediately.

4. Purée, and season with salt and pepper to taste.

Serving Size: 8

Vegetables

Robert Graham, "Self-Portrait
in Mashed Potatoes"...68

29 72 Market St. Mashed Potatoes.....................................69

30 Potatoes au Gratin...70

31 Celery Root Mousse..71

32 Eggplant and Bell Pepper Terrine
with Sun-Dried Tomato Vinaigrette..............................72

33 Warm Asparagus with
Carrot Tarragon Dressing...75

Sharon Truax and Derrik Van Nimwegen,
"Say Ahhhh!"..76

34 Fennel Ratatouille..77

Robert Graham, Artist - "Self-Portrait in Mashed Potatoes"
MASHED POTATOES

72 Market St. Mashed Potatoes

6 MEDIUM IDAHO RUSSET POTATOES, UNPEELED, CUT INTO 8 PIECES

1 TABLESPOON SALT

1 1/2 CUPS WHIPPING CREAM

4 TABLESPOONS BUTTER (1/2 STICK)

SALT AND PEPPER

1 Place the potatoes in a pot and add enough water to cover. Add the salt and bring to a boil. Reduce heat to low and simmer, covered, until soft, about 25 minutes.

2 Strain the potatoes, reserving 3 cups of the cooking liquid.

3 Rice the potatoes by pushing through a coarse strainer or sieve.

4 In a small saucepan, bring cream and butter just to a boil. Fold into the potatoes.

5 Add the potato liquid a little at a time, until the potatoes are the consistency you desire. Season with salt and pepper to taste.

Serving Size: 8

Some of the best dishes are the easiest to prepare — this is one of them! Many variations are possible. Try adding a layer of another vegetable between the potato layers, such as

Potatoes au Gratin

sautéed mushrooms, caramelized onion, even artichoke hearts.

1 TEASPOON BUTTER

1 TEASPOON CHOPPED GARLIC

2 CUPS WHIPPING CREAM

6 MEDIUM IDAHO RUSSET POTATOES, PEELED AND SLICED $1/8$-INCH THICK

SALT AND PEPPER

1 Preheat oven to 350 degrees.

2 Rub a flame-proof casserole dish with the butter and garlic.

3 Season the potatoes with salt and pepper to taste. Pour the cream into the dish. Layer the potatoes in the casserole in an overlapping spiral pattern on top of the cream, starting at the outside and working toward the center.

4 Bring the potatoes to a simmer over low heat on top of the stove.

5 When the cream begins to bubble, place the casserole in the oven and bake, uncovered, until golden brown, about 35 to 45 minutes. Allow to sit for 5 minutes before serving.

Serving Size: 8

A classic French side dish, excellent with rack of lamb or any grilled meat. A well-grown celery root, also called celeriac, is about the size of a grapefruit, lumpy and brown, firm to the touch.

Celery Root Mousse

2 CELERY ROOTS, PEELED AND
CUT INTO 1/2-INCH CUBES

1 TEASPOON LEMON JUICE

1 TEASPOON SALT

4 CUPS BOILING WATER

1/2 CUP WHIPPING CREAM

2 TABLESPOONS OLIVE OIL

SALT AND PEPPER

1   In a medium saucepan, combine celery root, lemon juice, and salt in the boiling water and bring back to a boil. Reduce heat to low and simmer, uncovered, for 10 minutes, until celery root is tender.

2   Strain, reserving 1/2 cup of the cooking liquid. Transfer celery root to a food processor.

3   Heat the cream until it starts to boil, then remove from heat immediately.

4   Using the steel blade, pulse celery root until puréed. With the motor running, slowly add the boiling cream.

5   With the motor still running, add the olive oil. If you prefer a thinner consistency, add the reserved cooking liquid. Season with salt and pepper to taste.

Serving Size: 8

Eggplant and Bell Pepper Terrine with Sun-Dried Tomato Vinaigrette

2 LARGE EGGPLANTS, SLICED
LENGTHWISE, 1/4-INCH THICK

3 MEDIUM ZUCCHINI, SLICED
LENGTHWISE, 1/4-INCH THICK

SALT AND PEPPER

4 TABLESPOONS OLIVE OIL

6 MEDIUM ONIONS, SLICED
1/8-INCH THICK

1 TEASPOON CHOPPED GARLIC

4 GREEN BELL PEPPERS

4 RED BELL PEPPERS

4 YELLOW BELL PEPPERS

1 TABLESPOON UNFLAVORED GELATIN

SUN-DRIED TOMATO VINAIGRETTE
(SEE RECIPE ON FACING PAGE)

1. Season the eggplant and zucchini with salt and pepper and brush with oil. Put the remaining oil in a sauté pan and heat. Add the eggplant and zucchini in batches and sauté over medium heat until tender and golden, approximately 1 minute per side. Remove from pan and drain on paper towels.

2. Add sliced onion to the oil in the sauté pan and sauté over medium heat, stirring occasionally, until caramelized to a deep golden brown, about 15 minutes.

3. Add the garlic and cook for 3 more minutes. Season with salt and pepper to taste.

4. To roast the peppers: Prepare barbecue or grill. Char the peppers over high heat until blackened. Put the charred peppers in a brown bag or cover tightly with a dish towel for a few minutes to steam. This will loosen the charred skin. Remove the skin and seeds, and cut into 3 or 4 lengthwise strips. Press down to flatten as much as possible.

5. To prepare the terrine pan: Lightly grease a 10-inch loaf pan or an aluminum mold. Cut parchment paper to cover insides and bottom of the pan to prevent sticking.

6. Preheat oven to 300 degrees.

7. To assemble the terrine: Starting with eggplant, alternate layers of eggplant, zucchini, green, red, and yellow bell peppers, and onions, sprinkling a pinch of gelatin on top of each layer. End with a layer of eggplant. Cover top with parchment paper and encase the entire pan in aluminum foil.

Continued on next page

Eggplant and Bell Pepper Terrine
with Sun-Dried Tomato Vinaigrette

Continued

8 Put the loaf pan or mold in a larger pan filled with 1 inch of boiling water and bake for 1 hour at 300 degrees.

9 Remove from oven and place a weight (such as another loaf pan filled with cans) on top of the mold to keep the layers in place. This will force the vegetables to drain. Pour off the liquid, then recover the terrine and chill for at least 4 hours, but preferably overnight.

10 Remove the terrine from the mold and slice into 1-inch portions. Serve with Sun-Dried Tomato Vinaigrette.

Serving Size: 10

This dressing is also excellent with sliced mozzarella cheese and tomatoes.

Sun-Dried Tomato Vinaigrette

2 CUPS OLIVE OIL

4 SPRIGS THYME

4 SPRIGS ROSEMARY

4 GARLIC CLOVES

1/2 CUP SUN-DRIED TOMATOES, DRAINED

1/2 CUP BALSAMIC VINEGAR

1 In a saucepan, heat the olive oil. Add the thyme, rosemary, and garlic, and cook over low heat about 8 minutes, or until the garlic is golden.

2 Add the sun-dried tomatoes and the balsamic vinegar, and remove from heat. Let stand at room temperature until cool.

3 To serve, drizzle over each slice of Eggplant and Bell Pepper Terrine.

Serving Size: 10

Carrot Tarragon Dressing

1 CUP WATER

1 CARROT, PEELED AND SLICED

1/4 TEASPOON SALT

2 TABLESPOONS SHERRY VINEGAR

1 TEASPOON CHOPPED FRESH TARRAGON

1/2 TEASPOON DIJON MUSTARD

1/2 CUP PEANUT OIL

SALT AND PEPPER

1. In a medium saucepan, bring the water to a boil and add the carrot and salt. Cook, uncovered, for 8 to 10 minutes, until the carrot is tender. Strain, reserving 1/2 cup of the liquid.

2. Transfer the carrots to a blender and add sherry vinegar, tarragon, Dijon mustard, and 1/4 cup of the cooking liquid. Blend on medium speed for 3 minutes.

3. While the motor is running, slowly add the oil. If you prefer a thinner dressing, add more of the cooking liquid, until dressing reaches the desired consistency. Season with salt and pepper to taste.

Serving Size: 6

Warm Asparagus with Carrot Tarragon Dressing

2 BUNCHES JUMBO ASPARAGUS, ABOUT 30 SPEARS

8 CUPS BOILING WATER

2 TEASPOONS SALT

CARROT TARRAGON DRESSING (SEE RECIPE ON FACING PAGE)

1 TABLESPOON CHOPPED CHIVES

1 Peel the asparagus and trim the ends.

2 Place the asparagus in boiling salted water and cook, covered, for 5 minutes, or until the tips are tender.

3 Remove the asparagus from the water and arrange on a serving plate. Drizzle with Carrot Tarragon Dressing and garnish with chopped chives.

Serving Size: 6

Sharon Truax, Art Dealer, and Derrik Van Nimwegen, Artist - "Say Ahhhhh!"
WARM ASPARAGUS WITH CARROT TARRAGON DRESSING
photographed by E.F. Kitchen

Fennel Ratatouille

1 TABLESPOON OLIVE OIL

1 CUP DICED FRESH FENNEL

$^1/_4$ CUP DICED ONION

$^1/_4$ CUP DICED CELERY

$^1/_4$ CUP DICED TOMATO

$^1/_2$ TEASPOON MINCED GARLIC

HERBES DE PROVENCE

SALT AND PEPPER

$^1/_4$ CUP RICH CHICKEN STOCK

1 Heat the oil in a sauté pan until very hot. Add the fennel, onion, celery, and tomato, and sauté for 10 minutes over medium heat.

2 Add the garlic and herbes de Provence, and sauté for an additional 3 minutes. Season with salt and pepper to taste.

3 Before serving, add as much of the rich chicken stock as desired to thin the ratatouille slightly.

Serving Size: 6

35 Vegetable Risotto 80

36 Seafood Risotto with Saffron 81

James Evans and Daniel Samakow,
"Your Place or Ours?" 82

37 Banana Squash Ravioli 83

38 Lobster and Green Onion Ravioli
with Herb Sauce 85

Dudley Moore, "Hitting the High Notes" 86

39 Farfalle with Fava Beans and
Mushroom Ragout 87

40 Fettuccine with Grilled Chicken and
Vegetables and Red Bell Pepper Pesto 88

Alexandra Keller, "The Shortest Distance
Between Two Points Is a Straight Line" 90

41 Swiss Chard Gnocchi with Sage Butter 91

Additional fresh seasonal vegetables may be added or substituted to satisfy your tastes.
We often use fennel, mushrooms and eggplant. The finished risotto should be creamy and
almost pourable, the rice somewhat chewy and firm.

Vegetable Risotto

3 TABLESPOONS EXTRA VIRGIN OLIVE OIL

1 MEDIUM ONION, FINELY DICED

2 CUPS RICE (PREFERABLY ARBORIO RICE)

PINCH OF SAFFRON

1 CUP WHITE WINE

4 CUPS VEGETABLE STOCK OR WATER

1 CARROT, FINELY DICED

1 ZUCCHINI, FINELY DICED

1 TURNIP, FINELY DICED

2 CELERY STALKS, FINELY DICED

1/2 CUP SUN-DRIED TOMATOES
PACKED IN OIL, DRAINED

1 TEASPOON SALT

1/2 TEASPOON PEPPER

2 TABLESPOONS BUTTER

2 TABLESPOONS CHOPPED PARSLEY

1/2 CUP GRATED PARMESAN CHEESE

1 Heat the oil in a large sauté pan. Add the onion, rice, and saffron, and sauté over medium heat for 3 to 5 minutes, or until the onion is translucent.

2 Add the wine and 2 cups of the stock and continue to simmer, uncovered, over medium heat, until the liquid is reduced by three-quarters, about 7 minutes. Stir occasionally to keep the risotto from sticking.

3 Add the remaining 2 cups of stock, the carrot, zucchini, turnip, celery, and sun-dried tomato, and simmer over low heat, uncovered, for 3 to 5 minutes, until all of the liquid is absorbed by the rice. Season with salt and pepper and stir in the butter and parsley.

4 Add the grated cheese, saving a little to sprinkle on top, and serve.

Serving Size: 6

Seafood Risotto with Saffron

3 TABLESPOONS EXTRA VIRGIN OLIVE OIL

1 MEDIUM ONION, FINELY DICED

2 CUPS RICE (PREFERABLY ARBORIO RICE)

PINCH OF SAFFRON

1 CUP WHITE WINE

4 CUPS FISH OR VEGETABLE SHOCK

18 LITTLENECK CLAMS

24 BLACK MUSSELS

1/2 POUND SQUID, CLEANED

1/4 CUP DICED CARROT

1/4 CUP DICED CELERY

1/4 CUP DICED ZUCCHINI

1 TEASPOON SALT

1/2 TEASPOON PEPPER

2 TABLESPOONS BUTTER

18 JUMBO SHRIMP, PEELED AND DEVEINED

1/2 POUND BAY SCALLOPS

1 TABLESPOON CHOPPED PARSLEY

1. Heat the oil in a large skillet. Add the onion, rice, and saffron, and sauté over medium heat for 3 to 5 minutes, or until the onion is translucent.

2. Add the white wine and 2 cups of the stock and continue to simmer, uncovered, over medium heat, about 2 to 3 minutes. Stir occasionally to keep risotto from sticking to the pan.

3. Add the remaining 2 cups of stock, the clams, mussels, squid, carrot, celery, and zucchini. Season with salt and pepper. Cover and simmer over low heat for about 7 minutes.

4. While the risotto is simmering, melt the butter in a separate pan. Add the shrimp and sauté for 2 minutes on each side. Add the bay scallops and sauté for an additional 2 minutes.

5. When the liquid in the risotto pan is mostly absorbed, stir the shrimp and scallops into the rice mixture. Add the parsley, cover, and simmer over low heat until all the liquid is absorbed, about 3 to 5 minutes. Serve immediately.

Serving Size: 6

James Evans and Daniel Samakow, Restaurateurs - "Your Place or Ours?"
BANANA SQUASH RAVIOLI
photographed by Christine Caldwell

Banana Squash Ravioli

FOR THE FILLING:

1 POUND BANANA SQUASH, SKINNED, SEEDED, AND DICED

SALT AND PEPPER

2 CUPS WATER

1 TABLESPOON HONEY

4 EGG YOLKS

4 TABLESPOONS BUTTER

$^1/_4$ CUP WHIPPING CREAM

FOR THE SAUCE:

$^1/_2$ CUP DISTILLED VINEGAR

$^1/_2$ CUP DRY WHITE WINE

10 PEPPERCORNS, CRACKED

2 SHALLOTS, FINELY CHOPPED

1 BUNCH TARRAGON, CHOPPED

$^1/_2$ CUP CHICKEN STOCK

2 TABLESPOONS BUTTER

RAVIOLI DOUGH (SEE RECIPE ON PAGE 84), OR 1 PACKAGE GYOZA SKINS

1 EGG YOLK BEATEN WTIH
1 TEASPOON WATER

1. Preheat the oven to 375 degrees.

2. For the filling: Season the diced squash with salt and pepper, and place in an ovenproof dish. Pour water over the squash. Bake at 375 degrees for approximately 25 minutes, or until it is easily pierced with a fork.

3. In a mixing bowl or blender, combine the cubes of squash, honey, egg yolks, butter, and cream, and beat until smooth. Set aside or refrigerate until ready to use.

4. To prepare the sauce: In a saucepan, combine the vinegar, wine, cracked peppercorns, shallots, and tarragon. Cook, stirring occasionally, over medium heat, until dry. Add the chicken stock and reduce by one-third. Season with salt if desired. Finish by adding butter and stirring until all ingredients are combined. Set aside or refrigerate until ready to use.

5. Roll the prepared ravioli dough on a floured surface to a thickness of $^1/_8$ inch. Cut into circles approximately 4 inches in diameter, or smaller, if you prefer a smaller ravioli. If using a pasta machine, use setting #6. If using gyoza skins, use the smaller squares if they are available, or use the large sheets and cut to size.

6. Place 1 tablespoon of the squash mixture in the center of each pasta circle and fold in half. Seal the edges by dipping a finger into the beaten egg yolk mixture and dabbing it on the edge of the pasta circle. Press the dough together to seal. Chill or freeze the pasta for at least 10 minutes, so that the dough becomes firm.

7. In a stockpot, bring 8 cups of water to a boil. Add the ravioli and boil for 3 minutes or until cooked through. Strain and serve with heated sauce.

Serving Size: 6

Ravioli Dough

2 1/2 CUPS ALL-PURPOSE FLOUR

2 EGGS

2 EGG YOLKS

1 TABLESPOON BUTTER, SOFTENED

1 1/2 TABLESPOONS HOT WATER

SALT

1. Put the flour in the bowl of an electric mixer. Using a paddle attachment, add the eggs and egg yolks one at a time, then the butter, then the hot water. Season with salt.

2. Mix the dough briefly, about 2 minutes, until it starts to pull away from the sides of the bowl. Do not overmix or the dough will become too elastic.

3. Form dough into a ball and cover with plastic. Chill for at least 2 hours before rolling.

Serving Size: 6

Lobster and Green Onion Ravioli with Herb Sauce

RAVIOLI DOUGH (SEE RECIPE ON FACING PAGE) OR 1 PACKAGE GOYOZA SKINS

FOR THE FILLING:

1 TABLESPOON BUTTER

1/4 CUP THINLY SLICED GREEN ONIONS, BOTH GREEN AND WHITE PARTS

1 POUND COOKED LOBSTER MEAT, FINELY DICED

SALT AND PEPPER

1 EGG YOLK, BEATEN WITH 1 TEASPOON WATER

FOR THE SAUCE:

1 CUP CHICKEN STOCK

2 TABLESPOONS CREAM OF RICE CEREAL

SALT AND PEPPER

2 TEASPOONS PARSLEY, STEMS REMOVED

1 TEASPOON TARRAGON, STEMS REMOVED

1 TEASPOON CHIVES, STEMS REMOVED

1 TEASPOON CHERVIL, STEMS REMOVED

1 TEASPOON BASIL, STEMS REMOVED

1. Prepare the ravioli dough according to recipe.

2. In a sauté pan, melt the butter and sauté the green onion for 3 minutes. Add the diced lobster meat. Season with salt and pepper, then cool.

3. On a floured surface, roll dough 1/8-inch thick and cut into 4-inch circles. If using a pasta machine, use setting #6. If using gyoza skins, use the smaller squares if they are available, or use the large sheets and cut to size. Make 36 circles.

4. Place about 1 tablespoon of the lobster and green onion mixture in the center of each pasta circle and fold in half. Seal the edges by dipping a finger in the egg yolk mixture and dabbing it on the edge of the pasta circle. Press to seal. Chill or freeze the pasta for at least 10 minutes before cooking so that the dough becomes firm.

5. To make the sauce: In a saucepan, bring the chicken stock to a boil. Reduce to a simmer and add the cream of rice. Add salt and pepper to taste, and cook, stirring, for 3 minutes. Cool and transfer to a blender.

6. In the same saucepan, blanch parsley in boiling water for 1 minute. Cool.

7. Transfer the thickened stock to a blender. Add the parsley, tarragon, chives, chervil, and basil to the thickened stock, and blend on medium for 2 minutes. Add more parsley if desired to enhance the color

8. In a stockpot, boil 6 quarts of water. Add the ravioli circles and cook for 4 minutes. While ravioli is cooking transfer herb sauce to a saucepan and heat over medium heat until warm.

9. When pasta is cooked, strain it, and serve with the herb sauce.

Serving Size: 6

Dudley Moore, Entertainer - "Hitting the High Notes"
FARFALLE WITH FAVA BEANS AND MUSHROOM RAGOUT
photographed by Danny Duchovny

Fava beans are at their best in early summer. Bright green, sweet and tender beans the shape of limas form inside five-to-seven-inch-long paler green, slightly hairy pods, a half a dozen or so to the pod. Combined with the mushroom ragout, they make this pasta a hearty vegetarian meal.

Farfalle with Fava Beans and Mushroom Ragout

FOR THE SAUCE:

2 TABLESPOONS EXTRA VIRGIN OLIVE OIL

1 TABLESPOON BUTTER

2 TABLESPOONS DICED SHALLOTS

1 1/2 CUPS DICED BUTTON MUSHROOMS

1 1/2 CUPS DICED SHIITAKE MUSHROOMS

1 1/2 CUPS DICED OYSTER MUSHROOMS

3 TABLESPOONS DICED PORCINI MUSHROOMS

1/2 CUP SUN-DRIED TOMATOES PACKED
IN OIL, DRAINED AND CUT INTO JULIENNE

1 GARLIC CLOVE, CHOPPED

1/2 CUP FRESH FAVA BEANS,
REMOVED FROM PODS

1/2 CUP VEGETABLE STOCK

1/4 CUP SORREL, CUT INTO JULIENNE

FOR THE PASTA:

4 QUARTS WATER

1 TEASPOON OLIVE OIL

1 TABLESPOON SALT

3/4 POUND FARFALLE PASTA

SALT AND PEPPER

1. Heat the olive oil and butter in a large sauté pan. Add the shallots, mushrooms, and sun-dried tomatoes and sauté for 5 minutes, or until all the liquid has evaporated.

2. Add the garlic and fava beans and sauté for 2 more minutes.

3. Add the vegetable stock and 2 tablespoons of the julienned sorrel, and remove from heat. Set aside.

4. In a stockpot, boil the water with the olive oil and salt. Add the farfalle pasta and cook for 8 minutes, or until pasta is al dente.

5. Strain the pasta and add to the mushroom ragout. Season with salt and pepper to taste.

6. Cook the pasta-ragout mixture over medium heat, stirring constantly, for 2 minutes, or until heated through. Top with the remainder of the sorrel, and serve immediately.

Serving Size: 6

Red Bell Pepper Pesto

3 ROASTED RED BELL PEPPERS

3 TABLESPOONS EXTRA VIRGIN OLIVE OIL

4 GARLIC CLOVES

$^1/_2$ CUP LOOSELY PACKED BASIL

1 TABLESPOON GRATED PARMESAN CHEESE

1. To make the Red Pepper Pesto: Roast the peppers by charring them over high heat on a barbecue or grill. Put the charred peppers in a brown bag or cover tightly with a dish towel for a few minutes to steam. This will loosen the charred skin. Remove the skin and seeds.

2. In a sauté pan, heat the extra virgin olive oil, and cook the garlic cloves over a low flame until light brown, about 4 minutes. Transfer to a food processor, and add the roasted red bell pepper, basil, and Parmesan cheese. Pulse until a smooth pesto is formed. Reserve.

A colorful and simple dish which can be served with or without the chicken. The Red Pepper Pesto can be prepared well in advance and kept chilled until ready to use.

Fettuccine with Grilled Chicken and Vegetables and Red Bell Pepper Pesto

FOR THE SAUCE:

3 WHOLE CHICKEN BREASTS,
BONED AND SKINNED

SALT AND PEPPER

1 CARROT, SLICED LENGTHWISE,
1/4-INCH THICK

1 ZUCCHINI, SLICED LENGTHWISE,
1/4-INCH THICK

1 SMALL EGGPLANT, UNPEELED,
SLICED IN STRIPS 1/4-INCH THICK

1 TABLESPOON OLIVE OIL

1 TEASPOON BUTTER

1 MEDIUM ONION, SLICED

1 CUP VEGETABLE STOCK OR WATER

1/2 CUP WHIPPING CREAM (OPTIONAL)

FOR THE PASTA:

1 1/2 POUNDS FETTUCCINE

6 QUARTS WATER

1 TABLESPOON CHOPPED PARSLEY

1. Heat the barbecue grill. Season the chicken breasts with salt and pepper. Grill over high heat until cooked through, about 10 to 12 minutes. Cool slightly, and cut into 1-inch cubes.

2. Brush the carrot, zucchini and eggplant with olive oil and season with salt and pepper. Grill the vegetables until cooked through, about 4 to 5 minutes. The carrot will take a little longer than the other vegetables. Dice into 1/4-inch cubes.

3. Heat the butter in a sauté pan and add the onion. Cook until light brown in color, about 7 minutes. In a large bowl, combine with grilled chicken and grilled vegetables and onions, and reserve.

4. In a large stockpot, heat 6 quarts of water.

5. While the water is heating, combine vegetable stock, reserved Red Pepper Pesto, cream (optional), and the grilled chicken and vegetable mixture in a large frying pan, and heat over a low flame.

6. When the water in the stockpot boils, add the fettuccine and cook until it is al dente, about 6 minutes. Strain, and add the noodles to the warmed sauce.

7. Top with chopped parsley, toss, and serve.

Serving Size: 6

Alexandra Keller - "The Shortest Distance Between Two Points Is a Straight Line"
FETTUCCINE WITH GRILLED CHICKEN AND VEGETABLES AND RED PEPPER PESTO
photograhed by Anne Kresl

These green gnocchi are much lighter than the usual potato version, so the finished dish virtually melts in your mouth. Unless the chard is very small, you will want to separate the leaves from their ribs before cutting into julienne. If you wish, you may dice and poach the stems and use them as a garnish.

Swiss Chard Gnocchi with Sage Butter

FOR THE GNOCCHI:

4 TABLESPOONS BUTTER

2 CUPS WATER

1 CUP ALL-PURPOSE FLOUR

2 CUPS SWISS CHARD, STEMS REMOVED AND CUT INTO JULIENNE

7 EGGS

8 CUPS WATER

FOR THE SAGE BUTTER:

2 TABLESPOONS BUTTER

2 TABLESPOONS CHOPPED SAGE

SALT AND PEPPER

1. Combine the butter and water in a saucepan. Bring to a boil.

2. Add the flour and swiss chard and mix well. Cook over low heat, stirring, for 7 to 10 minutes, until a ball of dough forms in the pan.

3. Transfer the mixture to a food processor, and while the motor is running, add the eggs through the feed tube. Blend until combined. Chill.

4. Bring the water to a boil in a large saucepan. Transfer the gnocchi mixture to a pastry bag. Drop several 1-inch pieces of the dough into the simmering water and cook for 1 minute. Remove from the water and continue cooking the rest of the gnocchi in batches until all are cooked. Chill until ready to serve.

5. In a sauté pan, heat 2 tablespoons of butter. Add the sage, and salt and pepper to taste.

6. When ready to serve, reheat the gnocchi by dropping them in boiling water for a few seconds. Remove from water and toss with sage butter.

Serving Size: 8

F i s h

72

Robert Fegan, "Catch of the Day".....................................94

42 Grilled Salmon with Dijon and Pommery
Mustard Sauce...95

Ed Moses, "In Rare Form".......................................96

43 Charred Peppered Rare Ahi Tuna with
Sautéed Spinach and Red Onion Soubise.................97

44 72 Market St. Bouillabaisse......................................98

Nate and Judy Chroman, and Marjorie Katz
"The Last Supper"..100

45 Seared Sea Scallops with Caramelized
Onions and Sweet and Sour Sauce...........................101

46 Baked Halibut with Wild Mushroom Crust
and Lentil Ragout 102

Joe DeAngelis, "Pumping Paella".........................104

47 72 Market St. Paella..105

Linda Stewart and Danny Duchovny,
"Two Shot"...106

48 72 Market St. Papillote..107

Robert Fegan, Waiter - "Catch of the Day"
GRILLED SALMON WITH DIJON AND POMMERY MUSTARD SAUCE
photographed by Ronald Cadiz

Another 72 favorite — this dish has been on the menu since the restaurant opened.

Because most salmon consumed in the United States is farmed rather than caught wild,

Grilled Salmon with Dijon
the flavor of the fish is consistent and it is available year-round.
and Pommery Mustard Sauce

3 POUNDS SALMON FILLET

SALT AND PEPPER

1 TABLESPOON OLIVE OIL

1 TABLESPOON BUTTER

2 TABLESPOONS FINELY CHOPPED SHALLOTS

1 GARLIC CLOVE, FINELY CHOPPED

1 BAY LEAF

PINCH OF PEPPER

1 CUP WHITE WINE

2 CUPS CHICKEN STOCK

1/2 CUP WHIPPING CREAM

1 TABLESPOON EXTRA STRONG
DIJON MUSTARD

1 TABLESPOON POMMERY
WHOLE-GRAIN MUSTARD

1 Light the barbecue grill. While coals are heating, cut the salmon fillet into six 8-ounce pieces, and season with salt and pepper. Brush the fish with oil and set aside.

2 Melt the butter in a saucepan, and add the shallots, garlic, bay leaf, and pepper. Sauté for 2 minutes, then add the white wine. Cook over high heat until reduced by half.

3 Add the chicken stock and reduce the liquid again by half.

4 Add the cream and both mustards. Reduce the heat to low and simmer the mixture, uncovered, until thick, about 5 minutes.

5 Grill the salmon for 4 minutes on each side. Spoon sauce onto the plate and set the salmon on top of it. Serve immediately.

Serving Size: 6

Ed Moses, Painter - "In Rare Form"
CHARRED PEPPERED RARE AHI TUNA WITH SAUTÉED SPINACH AND RED ONION SOUBISE
photographed by Pablo Aguilar

This is one of our signature dishes. Because ahi tuna is delicious served rare, you will want to select the finest, freshest fish. The best ahi is usually translucent, moist and shiny, and bright red in color.

Charred Peppered Rare Ahi Tuna with Sauteed Spinach and Red Onion Soubise

FOR THE SOUBISE:

1 TABLESPOON OLIVE OIL

1 MEDIUM RED ONION, DICED

1/2 CUP BALSAMIC VINEGAR

1 CUP CHICKEN STOCK

1 SPRIG FRESH THYME

1 BAY LEAF

SALT AND PEPPER

1 TEASPOON ARROWROOT

1 TABLESPOON WATER

2 1/2 POUNDS AHI TUNA

SALT AND FRESHLY CRACKED BLACK PEPPER

1 TABLESPOON EXTRA VIRGIN OLIVE OIL

2 GARLIC CLOVES

6 BUNCHES FRESH SPINACH, WASHED

1. For the Red Onion Soubise: Heat the oil in a sauté pan and add the onion. Sauté for 3 to 5 minutes, until the onion is translucent.

2. Add the vinegar, and cook over high heat until liquid is reduced to one quarter of the original amount.

3. Add the chicken stock, thyme and bay leaf, and season with salt and pepper to taste. Cook until reduced to one-half of the original amount.

4. Mix arrowroot with the water and add to the onion mixture to thicken. Remove the bay leaf, and correct seasonings if necessary. Set aside at room temperature, or chill until ready to serve.

5. Cut the ahi tuna into 6 steaks. Season each steak with salt and freshly cracked pepper.

6. Using a very hot cast-iron pan, sear the peppered tuna briefly on both sides. The tuna should be served very rare as this fish dries out when it is cooked too much.

7. For the spinach: Heat the olive oil in a large saucepan. Add the garlic cloves and sauté over medium-high heat until the garlic turns golden. Remove the garlic, and add the washed spinach (the leaves should still be damp), and cook until the spinach is wilted.

8. If the Red Onion Soubise has been chilled, bring it to room temperature. Serve the tuna on a bed of sautéed spinach, topped with the Red Onion Soubise.

Serving Size: 6

72 Market St. Bouillabaisse

FOR THE BROTH:

2 POUNDS FISH BONES,
PREFERABLY ROCKFISH

2 TABLESPOONS OLIVE OIL

2 LARGE ONIONS, SLICED

1 CARROT, SLICED

2 CELERY STALKS, SLICED

6 GARLIC CLOVES, SLICED

1 FENNEL BULB, SLICED

1/4 TEASPOON SAFFRON

2 SPRIGS FRESH THYME

1/2 BAY LEAF

3 PARSLEY STEMS

4 ROMA TOMATOES, PEELED,
SEEDED, AND SLICED

2 CUPS WHITE WINE

2 QUARTS WATER

SALT AND PEPPER

1 Rinse the fish bones.

2 Heat the olive oil in a stockpot. Add the fish bones, sliced onion, carrot, celery, garlic, fennel, saffron, thyme, bay leaf, and parsley stems, and sauté for 15 minutes, or until most of the liquid has evaporated.

3 Add the tomatoes and white wine and simmer, uncovered, for 5 more minutes.

4 Add 2 quarts of water to the pot and bring to a boil; simmer for 20 more minutes. Season with salt and pepper to taste.

5 Press the mixture through a sieve, allowing some of the thickness to seep through to create a richer broth. Strain a second time to make sure none of the fish bones have gone through the sieve into the strained stock.

Continued on next page

72 Market St. Bouillabaisse

FOR THE FISH AND VEGETABLES:

2 TABLESPOONS OLIVE OIL

2 CELERY STALKS, CUT INTO JULIENNE

2 LEEKS, WHITE PART ONLY,
CUT INTO JULIENNE

1 CARROT, CUT INTO JULIENNE

1 MEDIUM ONION, SLICED

1 FENNEL BULB, CUT INTO JULIENNE

PINCH OF SAFFRON

6 GARLIC CLOVES, CHOPPED FINE

SALT AND PEPPER

1 POUND JOHN DORY

1 POUND NEW ZEALAND RED SNAPPER

1 POUND MONKFISH

12 LITTLENECK CLAMS

18 BLACK MUSSELS

6 JUMBO SHRIMP

6 JUMBO SCALLOPS

Continued

6 While the stock is cooking, heat 2 tablespoons of olive oil in a sauté pan. Add the julienned celery, leek, carrot, onion, fennel, saffron, and chopped garlic, and cook until soft, about 5 minutes. Season with salt and pepper to taste, and reserve.

7 To prepare the fish: slice the John Dory, the snapper, and the monkfish into 2- to 3-ounce pieces. Reserve.

8 When almost ready to serve, add the clams to the stock. Simmer for 4 to 5 minutes, or until all the shellfish have opened.

9 Add the John Dory, snapper, monkfish, and the vegetable mixture to the stock. Bring to a simmer and add the mussels, shrimp, and scallops. Simmer for 2 more minutes and serve.

Serving Size: 6

Nate and Judy Chroman and Marjorie Katz, Wine Connoisseurs - "The Last Supper"
72 MARKET ST. BOUILLABAISSE
photographed by Pablo Aguilar

Traditionally, sea scallops have come from the Atlantic Coast. But in recent years they have begun being cultivated in California. As with all seafood, freshness is the most essential quality. Look for scallops that are cream colored or slightly pink and have an appealing sheen.

Seared Sea Scallops with Caramelized Onions and Sweet and Sour Sauce

FOR THE SAUCE:

¾ CUP RED WINE VINEGAR

5 TABLESPOONS HONEY

1¼ CUPS RED WINE

¾ CUP VEAL STOCK OR DEMI-GLACE

4 TABLESPOONS BUTTER

4 MEDIUM ONIONS, FINELY DICED

1 TEASPOON SUGAR (OPTIONAL)

2½ POUNDS JUMBO SEA SCALLOPS (ABOUT 36)

SALT AND PEPPER

2 TABLESPOONS CHOPPED CHIVES

1 For the sweet and sour sauce: In a saucepan, combine the vinegar and the honey. Cook, uncovered, over medium heat, until the liquid is reduced by half.

2 Add the wine. Continue cooking until the remaining liquid is reduced by one-third.

3 Add the veal stock or demi-glace. Simmer for 20 minutes. Strain and set aside.

4 In a sauté pan over medium heat, melt 2 tablespoons of butter. Add the onions and the sugar (if you desire a sweeter onion), and sauté until golden brown, about 10 minutes.

5 In another pan, melt the remaining 2 tablespoons butter. Season the sea scallops with salt and pepper, and sauté them in the butter, over medium heat, for 3 minutes on each side, or until cooked through.

6 To serve, rewarm the sweet and sour sauce. Spoon six dollops of sauce onto each plate, and top with ½ tablespoon of the onion mixture. Place a scallop on top of each dollop of caramelized onions. Garnish with chopped chives.

Serving Size: 6

Two species of halibut are found along the Pacific Coast, California halibut and Pacific halibut. Either variety will be delicious in this recipe. The lentil ragout provides a contrast in texture, color and flavor to the fish. Rinse lentils well before cooking. There is sometimes a grain or two of gravel mixed in the package!

Baked Halibut with Wild Mushroom Crust and Lentil Ragout

FOR THE LENTIL RAGOUT:

1 LARGE YELLOW ONION, CHOPPED

1 TABLESPOON BUTTER

10 OUNCES GREEN LENTILS

2 GARLIC CLOVES, CHOPPED

1 SPRIG THYME

1/2 BAY LEAF

2 TABLESPOONS ITALIAN PARSLEY,
STEMS ONLY

WATER OR CHICKEN STOCK

SALT AND PEPPER

FOR THE FISH:

2 1/4 POUNDS HALIBUT

1 TABLESPOON BUTTER
(OR MORE IF NEEDED)

SALT AND PEPPER

1 CUP WHITE WINE

1 For the Lentil Ragout: In a large sauté pan, sweat the onion in the butter until soft, about 3 to 5 minutes. Add the lentils and garlic.

2 With a piece of string, tie the thyme, bay leaf, and parsley stems together to make a bouquet garni and add to the sauté pan. Add enough water or chicken stock to cover, about 3 cups.

3 Season the mixture with salt and pepper, and cook, covered, over medium heat for 30 minutes, or until the lentils are tender and most of the water is absorbed. Remove the bouquet garni, but do not drain.

4 While the ragout is cooking, rinse the halibut and cut it into 6 steaks. Butter the bottom of a shallow pan and place the halibut in it. Season the fish with salt and pepper. Add the wine to the pan.

5 Preheat the oven to 350 degrees.

Continued on next page

Baked Halibut with Wild Mushroom Crust and Lentil Ragout

FOR THE CRUST:

1 SLICE WHITE BREAD, OR 1 CUP PREPARED BREADCRUMBS

$1/4$ CUP FINELY DICED BUTTON MUSHROOMS

$1/4$ CUP FINELY DICED SHIITAKE MUSHROOMS

$1/4$ CUP FINELY DICED CÈPES, FRESH OR FROZEN

2 SHALLOTS, FINELY CHOPPED

2 TEASPOONS FINELY CHOPPED CHIVES

1 TEASPOON FINELY CHOPPED TARRAGON

$1/2$ TEASPOON FINELY CHOPPED CHERVIL

2 TABLESPOONS FINELY CHOPPED PARSLEY

2 TABLESPOONS WHIPPING CREAM

SALT AND PEPPER

Continued

6. To make the mushroom crust: Place the bread in the bowl of a food processor and process until coarsely chopped. It should make about 1 cup.

7. In a mixing bowl, combine the breadcrumbs, mushrooms, shallots, chives, tarragon, chervil, parsley, and cream, and mix until thoroughly incorporated. Season with salt and pepper to taste.

8. Spread the mushroom crust mixture on top of the slices of halibut and bake at 350 degrees until cooked through, about 6 minutes.

9. To serve, warm the lentil ragout, spoon it onto serving plates, and put the crusted halibut on top of it.

Serving Size: 6

Joe DeAngelis, Mr. Universe and Mr. World - "Pumping Paella"
72 MARKET ST. PAELLA
photographed by Danny Duchovny

It is easier to prepare this dish in a traditional paella pan if you have one, but any large, sturdy shallow pan may be used instead. Try cooking it the traditional Spanish way, on a grill at an outdoor barbecue.

72 Market St. Paella

^{1}/2 CUP OLIVE OIL

1 MEDIUM ONION, FINELY DICED

3 MEDIUM GREEN BELL PEPPERS, FINELY DICED

^{1}/2 POUND DRY CHORIZO, THINLY SLICED

PINCH OF SAFFRON

6 GARLIC CLOVES, CHOPPED

2 CUPS GREEN PEAS, SHELLED

2 CUPS (ABOUT 1 POUND) BABY ARTICHOKES, TRIMMED AND QUARTERED

6 ROMA TOMATOES, PEELED, SEEDED AND DICED

1 POUND ARBORIO RICE

1 POUND CALAMARI, SLICED INTO ^{1}/2-INCH RINGS

1 CUP WHITE WINE

4 CUPS WATER

SALT

CAYENNE PEPPER

12 LITTLENECK CLAMS, SCRUBBED

1 POUND BLACK MUSSELS (ABOUT 3 CUPS), SCRUBBED

12 JUMBO SHRIMP (ABOUT 1^1/4 POUNDS), SHELLED AND DEVEINED

1. In a paella pan or large skillet, heat the olive oil and add the onion, bell pepper, chorizo, and saffron, and sauté for 5 minutes.

2. Add the garlic, peas, artichoke, tomato, and rice. Sauté for another 5 minutes.

3. Add the calamari and the wine. Bring to a boil, and cook until the liquid is absorbed. Add the water and bring back to a boil. Season with salt and cayenne pepper to taste.

4. Add the clams, mussels, and shrimp. Reduce heat to medium and cook, uncovered, for 10 to 12 minutes, or until the shellfish have opened and the liquid has evaporated.

Serving Size: 6

Linda Stewart, Producer, and Danny Duchovny, Director - "Two Shot"
72 MARKET ST. PAPILLOTE
photographed by Danny Duchovny

A very light and lovely meal which can be prepared ahead and simply placed in the oven fifteen minutes before you are ready to serve. Caution your guests that when the papillote is cut open, the escaping steam is very hot!

72 Market St. Papillote

3 OUNCES OLIVE OIL

1 ONION, CUT INTO JULIENNE

1 CARROT, CUT INTO JULIENNE

2 OUNCES SHIITAKE MUSHROOMS,
CUT INTO JULIENNE

1 LEEK, CUT INTO JULIENNE

1 CELERY STALK, CUT INTO JULIENNE

4 GARLIC CLOVES, CHOPPED

1 TEASPOON CHOPPED FRESH GINGER

1 CUP COOKED CANNELLINI BEANS

SALT AND PEPPER

1/2 POUND JUMBO SCALLOPS

1/2 POUND LARGE SHRIMP,
PEELED AND DEVEINED

1/2 POUND NEW ZEALAND RED SNAPPER

1. Heat 2 ounces of the the olive oil in a sauté pan and sauté the onion, carrot, mushrooms, leek, and celery until the onions are translucent.

2. Add the garlic, ginger, and cannellini beans. Season with salt and pepper to taste, and set aside to cool.

3. Cut parchment paper into eight 12-inch circles. Brush the papers with remaining 1 ounce of oil.

4. Preheat the oven to 350 degrees.

5. Place one-fourth of the vegetable mixture in the center of each of four of the circles. Top each with a portion of the scallops, shrimp, and snapper.

6. Place another circle on top of each of the four filled circles and roll edges to seal.

7. Place on a large cookie sheet and bake at 350 degrees for 12 minutes.

Serving Size: 4

F o w l

Helena Kallianiotes, "Zesty"......................................110

49 Grilled Marinated Chicken
    with Tomatillo Salsa...............................111

*Steve Ferguson, "Concerto for Chicken
and Apples"*..112

50 Chicken with Caramelized Apples
    and Calvados..113

Helen Bartlett and Tony Bill, "Fowl Play"..................114

51 Chicken Stuffed with Tarragon Mousse
    in a Sea Urchin Sauce...............................115

52 Roasted Squab with Candied Garlic
    and Green Lentil Ragout..............................116

53 Muscovy Duck with Port Wine Sauce.......................118

54 Crispy Air-Dried Duck with Pear
    and Mint Sauce..119

Robert Lia and Canoah, "Main Squeeze"..................120

55 Ed Landry's Quail Gumbo...............................121

Helena Kallianiotes, Impresario - "Zesty"
GRILLED MARINATED CHICKEN WITH TOMATILLO SALSA
photographed by Pablo Aguilar

Tomatillos are native to Mexico, and it may surprise you to know that they are not related to tomatoes. In this warm salsa, they add a nice bite to the simple grilled chicken. The salsa can be prepared ahead and chilled, then rewarmed just before serving.

Grilled Marinated Chicken with Tomatillo Salsa

2 WHOLE CHICKENS, DEBONED AND QUARTERED

¹/₄ CUP OLIVE OIL

1 TABLESPOON CHOPPED GARLIC

2 TABLESPOONS CHOPPED OREGANO

FOR THE TOMATILLO SALSA:

¹/₂ POUND TOMATILLOS

¹/₄ CUP CHAMPAGNE WINE VINEGAR

¹/₄ TEASPOON GROUND CUMIN

¹/₄ TEASPOON CHOPPED OREGANO

¹/₄ TEASPOON PEPPER

³/₄ TEASPOON CHOPPED GARLIC

1 JALAPEÑO, SEEDED AND CHOPPED

¹/₂ BUNCH GREEN ONIONS, CHOPPED

¹/₄ BUNCH CILANTRO, CHOPPED

SALT

1. Lay the chicken quarters in a large, shallow dish.

2. Combine the olive oil, garlic, and oregano in a small mixing bowl. Pour over the chicken, cover tightly, and chill for 12 hours.

3. To prepare the salsa: Remove the hulls from the tomatillos and dice.

4. Combine the tomatillos with vinegar, cumin, oregano, black pepper, garlic, and jalapeño in a saucepan. Simmer over low heat for 10 minutes.

5. Transfer tomatillo mixture to a blender and purée. Add the green onion, cilantro, and salt to taste.

6. Which chicken is fully marinated, heat the barbecue grill. When it is hot, brush it lightly with a wire brush. Then, using a rag, lightly season the grill with oil to help reduce sticking.

7. Bring the chicken to room temperature before cooking. Grill over high heat for 10 to 12 minutes or until cooked through.

8. While chicken is cooking, heat the Tomatillo Salsa. Serve hot.

Serving Size: 4

Steve Ferguson, Pianist - "Concerto for Chicken and Apples"
CHICKEN WITH CARAMELIZED APPLES AND CALVADOS
photographed by E.K. Waller

Chicken with Caramelized Apples and Calvados

A simple but dramatic change-of-pace chicken dish. The tartness of the Granny Smith apples contrasts nicely with the sweetness of the Calvados. When adding the liqueur, the sauce may flame, so pour it slowly and with care.

6 WHOLE CHICKEN BREASTS, DEBONED

2 1/2 TABLESPOONS BUTTER

3 GRANNY SMITH APPLES, PEELED, CORED, AND SLICED 1/4-INCH THICK

1/4 CUP CALVADOS

1/2 CUP WHIPPING CREAM

SALT AND PEPPER

1. Preheat the oven to 400 degrees.

2. In a large frying pan, sauté the chicken breasts in 1 tablespoon of the butter for 2 minutes on each side.

3. Place the breasts skin side down in an ovenproof dish, and bake at 400 degrees for 7 to 10 minutes, until juices run clear when pierced with a fork.

4. While the chicken is cooking, melt 1 tablespoon of the butter in a saucepan. Add the apple slices and sauté for 5 minutes, or until golden brown. If needed, add up to 1/2 tablespoon additional butter.

5. Add the Calvados and cook over high heat until reduced by half.

6. Add the cream, and simmer for 2 more minutes. Season with salt and pepper to taste.

7. Remove the chicken from the oven and transfer to serving plates. Spoon the apples and sauce over the chicken, and serve.

Serving Size: 6

Helen Bartlett, Producer, and Tony Bill, Director - "Fowl Play"
CHICKEN STUFFED WITH TARRAGON MOUSSE IN A SEA URCHIN SAUCE
photographed by Danny Duchovny

Chicken Stuffed with Tarragon Mousse in a Sea Urchin Sauce

6 WHOLE CHICKEN BREASTS, DEBONED

1 TEASPOON CHOPPED SHALLOTS

1 TABLESPOON TARRAGON LEAVES

$1/2$ CUP WHIPPING CREAM

1 EGG YOLK

FOR THE SEA URCHIN SAUCE:

1 TEASPOON FINELY CHOPPED SHALLOTS

$1^1/2$ TEASPOONS BUTTER

$1/2$ CUP WHITE WINE

$1/2$ CUP VEGETABLE OR CHICKEN STOCK

$1/2$ CUP WHIPING CREAM

1 TEASPOON CREAM OF RICE CEREAL

6 PIECES SEA URCHIN ROE

SALT AND PEPPER

1. To prepare the Chicken Tarragon Mousse: Remove the skin from two of the chicken breasts and discard. Place the two skinless breasts in a food processor, and process with the steel blade until smooth.

2. Add the shallots, tarragon, cream, and egg yolk, and pulse for 1 minute. Cover and chill until ready to use.

3. Cut pockets in the middle of each of the remaining four breasts, being careful not to break through the sides of the meat.

4. Put the mousse into a pastry bag and pipe it into each of the four cut breasts. Cover and chill until ready to cook.

5. Preheat the oven to 400 degrees.

6. While the oven is heating, make the sauce: In a saucepan, sauté the shallots in $1/2$ teaspoon of the butter for 2 minutes. Add the white wine and reduce by half. Add the chicken or vegetable stock and again reduce by half. Add the cream and the cream of rice cereal, and return to a boil.

7. Reduce the heat and simmer, whisking constantly, for 2 minutes. Transfer sauce to a blender and blend on high for 3 minutes.

8. With the motor running, slowly add the sea urchin roe. Season with salt and pepper to taste and reserve.

9. In a sauté pan, melt the remaining 1 teaspoon of butter. Sauté the four stuffed chicken breasts for 2 minutes on each side.

10. Place the breasts skin side down in an ovenproof pan, and bake at 400 degrees for 7 to 10 minutes, or until chicken is cooked through.

11. Transfer to a serving plate, spoon the sauce over the chicken, and serve.

Serving Size: 4

Some of the best green lentils come from Le Puy, a town in the mountainous French region of Haute-Loire. They are available in specialty food stores and are well worth the extra effort it may take to find them. Rinse the lentils well before cooking.

Roasted Squab with Candied Garlic and Green Lentil Ragout

FOR THE LENTIL RAGOUT:

4 CUPS WATER OR CHICKEN STOCK

1 CUP GREEN LENTILS, RINSED AND PICKED OVER

1 WHOLE CARROT

1 MEDIUM ONION, QUARTERED

1 CELERY STALK

1 BAY LEAF

2 GARLIC CLOVES

SALT AND PEPPER

2 TABLESPOONS BUTTER

FOR THE SQUAB:

1 TABLESPOON BUTTER

6 WHOLE SQUAB

SALT AND PEPPER

1 To prepare the lentils: In a stockpot, combine the water or chicken stock, lentils, carrot, onion, celery, bay leaf and 2 garlic cloves. Bring to a boil, then reduce heat to low and simmer, covered, for 25 minutes, or until the lentils are soft. Season with salt and pepper to taste. Remove vegetables and garlic, and stir in 2 tablespoons butter. Keep warm.

2 To prepare the squab: Preheat the oven to 350 degrees. In a large skillet, melt 1 tablespoon butter. Season the squab with salt and pepper on each side and place breast side down in the skillet. Sear over high heat for 45 seconds on each side or until golden brown. Remove squabs and arrange on their backs in an ovenproof dish. Roast, uncovered, at 350 degrees for 12 minutes.

Continued on next page

Roasted Squab with Candied Garlic and Green Lentil Ragout

FOR THE CANDIED GARLIC:

2 CUPS WATER

16 GARLIC CLOVES, PEELED

1/2 CUP EXTRA VIRGIN OLIVE OIL

Continued

3 To candy the garlic: Boil 2 cups of water. Blanch the 16 garlic cloves by adding them to the pot and returning it to a boil. Immediately remove the pan from heat and strain the garlic under cold water.

4 In a sauté pan, heat the extra virgin olive oil. Add the blanched garlic and cook over medium heat for 5 minutes, or until golden brown. Stir into the lentil ragout.

5 Remove the squab from the oven and let rest for 5 minutes on top of stove. If desired, debone squab as you would a small chicken.

6 To serve, reheat the candied garlic and green lentil ragout. Put a portion of the ragout on each plate and top with a squab and 4 garlic cloves.

Serving Size: 4

Muscovy Duck with Port Wine Sauce

The flesh of Muscovy duck is a deep red color and has a richer flavor than traditional duck. The sweetness and color of the port wine sauce creates a dish that is festive without being overly rich. If demi-glace is not available from your specialty grocer, you may substitute veal stock, or e-mail us and we will send you the recipe.

2 MUSCOVY DUCK BREASTS, TRIMMED
AND CLEANED

SALT AND PEPPER

1 TABLESPOON BUTTER

1 TEASPOON CHOPPED SHALLOTS

1/2 CUP PORT WINE

3/4 CUP DEMI-GLACE

1. Preheat the oven to 375 degrees.

2. Heat a sauté pan until very hot. Season the duck breasts with salt and pepper on the meat side only, and place them skin side down in the sauté pan. Sear, turning on all sides.

3. Put the meat skin side down in an ovenproof dish and bake at 375 degrees for 8 to 10 minutes, until flesh is just pink. Let stand while preparing the sauce.

4. In the same sauté pan that the duck breasts cooked in, combine the butter and shallots, and sauté until the shallots are translucent.

5. Add the port carefully, as the pan will flame when the alcohol is added, and reduce by one-half. Add the demi-glace and reduce again by half.

6. Season sauce with salt and pepper to taste, and keep warm while slicing the duck.

7. Thinly slice the duck and spread it into a fan shape on the plate. Serve with the sauce spooned around the sides.

Serving Size: 4

Crispy Air-Dried Duck with Pear and Mint Sauce

Air-dried duck and plum wine can be found in any Asian market. Be sure to let the duck sit at room temperature for at least 5 hours before cooking so the fat will soften and melt off when the dish is cooked. It is also essential to loosen the duck skin from the flesh before cooking in order for the fat to melt fully.

2 AIR-DRIED DUCKS OR
LONG ISLAND DUCKLINGS

FOR THE PEAR AND MINT SAUCE:

2 WHOLE CLOVES

5 WHOLE PEPPERCORNS

1 CINNAMON STICK

1 CUP RED WINE

1 CUP PLUM WINE

1/2 CUP CHICKEN STOCK

5 PEARS, PEELED AND CORED

2 TABLESPOONS CHOPPED MINT

1. Remove the duck from its wrapping and let sit at room temperature for 5 hours.

2. Preheat the oven to 375 degrees.

3. Place the duck on a rack in an ovenproof dish. Using your fingers, loosen the duck's skin away from the flesh. Place in the oven and cook for 1 1/2 to 2 hours, turning every 30 minutes so the breast, back and both sides become very well-browned. Remove from the oven and let cool.

4. While duck is cooking, prepare the sauce: Tie the cloves, peppercorns, and cinnamon stick inside a piece of cheesecloth.

5. In a saucepan, bring the red wine, plum wine, chicken stock, pears, and the cheesecloth bundle to a boil. Simmer, uncovered, over low heat, for 15 minutes.

6. Remove the cheesecloth bundle and transfer the liquid to a blender. Purée until smooth, then add the chopped mint. Reserve at room temperature until duck is cooked.

7. When duck is cooked, remove the flesh from the carcass and place in the oven for an additional 7 to 10 minutes.

8. Spread Pear and Mint Sauce on serving plates and top with the duck.

Serving Size: 4

119

Robert Lia, Chef, and Canoah - "Main Squeeze"
CRISPY AIR-DRIED DUCK WITH PEAR AND MINT SAUCE
photographed by Ronald Cadiz

Ed Landry's Quail Gumbo

1 CARROT, CHOPPED

1 CELERY STALK, CHOPPED

1 MEDIUM ONION, CHOPPED

2 TABLESPOONS OLIVE OIL

1 TURKEY LEG AND THIGH

2 QUARTS WATER

3 TABLESPOONS OLIVE OIL

3 TABLESPOONS ALL-PURPOSE FLOUR

1/2 CUP DICED CELERY

1/2 CUP DICED ONION

1/2 CUP DICED GREEN BELL PEPPER

1 TEASPOON MINCED GARLIC

1 TABLESPOON TOMATO PASTE

SALT AND PEPPER

CAYENNE PEPPER

1/2 TEASPOON CHOPPED OREGANO

1/2 TEASPOON CHOPPED THYME

1 CUP COOKED WILD RICE

2 TABLESPOONS PLAIN YOGURT

SALT

CAYENNE PEPPER

4 QUAIL

1 TABLESPOON BUTTER

1/4 TEASPOON TABASCO SAUCE

2 TEASPOONS GUMBO FILÉ

1. In a large stockpot, sauté the chopped carrot, celery, and onion with 2 tablespoons of olive oil, until the onion is translucent.

2. Add the turkey thigh and leg and 2 quarts of water and bring to a boil. Reduce the heat and simmer, covered, approximately 2 hours, or until the stock is reduced by one-half. Remove the turkey meat from the water and debone. Reserve for later use. Strain the liquid and reserve.

3. In the same stockpot, heat the 3 tablespoons of olive oil and whisk in the flour to make a roux. Cook over low to medium heat until the roux is dark brown, stirring constantly.

4. Add the diced celery, onion, and bell pepper, and sauté until the onion is translucent.

5. Add the garlic and sauté for 1 minute. Add the turkey stock and the tomato paste, and bring to a boil. Season with salt and pepper and cayenne to taste. Add the oregano and thyme. Reduce stock to a simmer.

6. Add 1/2 of the reserved deboned turkey to the stock mixture. Mix the other half of the turkey with the wild rice and yogurt. Season with salt and cayenne pepper to taste. Stuff the quail with the rice mixture.

7. Preheat the oven to 375 degrees. Season the outside of the quail with salt. Heat 1 tablespoon of butter in a sauté pan and brown the breast side of the quail. Place in the oven and cook for 10 minutes.

8. While the quail is cooking, finish the gumbo by adjusting the seasoning. Then add the gumbo filé and tabasco. (Do not boil after filé has been added or the soup will become ropy.) When quail is cooked, spoon gumbo into a bowl and place the stuffed quail on top.

Serving Size: 4

Meats

72

Leonard Schwartz, "From Market St.
to Maple Dr." 122

56 72 Market St. Meat Loaf and Gravy 125

The Venice Family Clinic Art Walk,
"Kicking Ass at the Art Walk" 126

57 72 Market St. Kick Ass Chili
and Corn Muffins 127

58 Osso Buco 129

Andy Nevill and Mark Steffen,
"Tattoo To Go" 130

59 Veal Chop with Porcini Mushrooms
and Sweet Potato Purée 131

60 Sweetbread and Lobster Chartreuse
with Pea Coulis 132

Bear, "I've got a bone to pick. . ." 134

61 Grilled Pork Chop with Tomato
Ginger Chutney 135

62 Roasted Rack of Lamb with Orange
and Juniper Berry Crust 136

Meat Loaf Gravy

2 TABLESPOONS BUTTER

4 SHALLOTS, MINCED

1 SPRIG THYME

1 BAY LEAF

DASH OF CRUSHED PEPPERCORNS

$^1/_4$ CUP CHOPPED RED BELL PEPPERS

$^1/_4$ CUP CHOPPED YELLOW BELL PEPPERS

1 CUP DRY WHITE WINE

1 CUP VEAL OR BEEF STOCK

1 CUP CHICKEN STOCK

2 ROMA TOMATOES, PEELED, SEEDED, AND DICED

SALT AND PEPPER

1. In a heavy pan, melt 1 tablespoon of the butter, and sauté the shallots, thyme, bay leaf, peppercorns, and red and yellow bell peppers over medium-high heat for 3 minutes.

2. Add the wine and simmer over high heat until reduced by three-fourths, to make a glaze.

3. Add the veal stock and chicken stock, and simmer, uncovered, over high heat until reduced by one-fourth.

4. Add the tomatoes and bring to a slow simmer. Cook, covered, for 20 minutes.

5. Stir in the remaining 1 tablespoon of butter and season with salt and pepper to taste.

6. Strain, discarding bay leaf and thyme before serving.

Serving Size: 10

This recipe by 72's first chef, Leonard Schwartz, remains the restaurant's most popular dish. After you try it we are certain it will become one of your favorites at home as well.

72 Market St. Meat Loaf

It's also great for sandwiches too!

1 TABLESPOON BUTTER

3/4 CUP MINCED GREEN ONION

3/4 CUP MINCED WHITE ONION

1/2 CUP MINCED CARROT

1/2 CUP MINCED CELERY

1/4 CUP MINCED RED BELL PEPPER

1/4 CUP MINCED GREEN BELL PEPPER

2 TEASPOONS MINCED GARLIC

1 TEASPOON SALT

1 TEASPOON PEPPER

1/2 TEASPOON CAYENNE PEPPER

1/2 TEASPOON NUTMEG

1/2 TEASPOON CUMIN

3 EGGS, BEATEN

1/2 CUP KETCHUP

1/2 CUP HALF AND HALF

1 1/2 POUNDS LEAN GROUND BEEF

1/2 POUND LEAN GROUND PORK SAUSAGE,
WITH NO HERBS OR SEASONINGS ADDED

3/4 CUP PREPARED BREADCRUMBS

MEAT LOAF GRAVY
(SEE RECIPE ON FACING PAGE)

1. Preheat the oven to 350 degrees.

2. Heat the butter in a heavy skillet and add the green onion, white onion, carrots, celery, red bell pepper, green bell pepper, and garlic. Cook, stirring often, for 10 minutes, or until the moisture has evaporated. Cool.

3. In a large mixing bowl, combine the salt, pepper, cayenne pepper, nutmeg, cumin, and eggs and mix well. Add the ketchup and half and half. Blend thoroughly.

4. Add the ground beef, ground pork, breadcrumbs, and the vegetable mixture. It might be easier to mix this with your hands.

5. Grease a loaf pan and add the meat mixture, pressing it into the corners. Put the loaf pan in a larger pan filled 1-inch-high with boiling water. Cook at 350 degrees for 45 to 60 minutes. Let rest for 10 minutes before serving. Serve with Meat Loaf Gravy.

Serving Size: 6

Corn Muffins

2 TABLESPOONS CUMIN

2 CUPS ALL-PURPOSE FLOUR

1 TEASPOON SALT

1/4 CUP BAKING POWDER

13 GREEN ONIONS, CHOPPED

4 GREEN BELL PEPPERS, CHOPPED

2²/3 CUPS SOUR CREAM

2²/3 CUPS MILK

4 EGGS

5 TABLESPOONS SOFTENED BUTTER

3¹/3 CUPS CORN KERNELS,
CUT OFF THE COB, OR FROZEN

1³/8 CUPS YELLOW CORNMEAL

1 TABLESPOON CRUSHED RED PEPPER FLAKES

3/4 CUP GRATED CHEDDAR CHEESE

1. Preheat the oven to 350 degrees.

2. Sift together the cumin, flour, salt, and baking powder and set aside.

3. In a large mixing bowl, combine the green onion, green bell pepper, sour cream, milk, eggs, and butter. Mix until thoroughly combined.

4. Add the corn, cornmeal, crushed red pepper, and cheese. Fold in the flour mixture and mix until incorporated. Do not overmix.

5. Pour into greased muffin tins and bake at 350 degrees for 20 minutes or until lightly browned. Serve warm.

Serving Size: 20 muffins

Another 72 original — not for the faint of heart! For events such as the Venice Family
Clinic Art Walk, we make it in batches big enough to serve five hundred people! Don't
72 Market St. Kick Ass Chili
forget that the Corn Muffins are equally delicious and just as spicy.

1/2 POUND BACON

3 POUNDS PORK BUTT, CUT INTO 1-INCH CUBES

1/4 CUP PEANUT OIL

3 POUNDS BEEF SIRLOIN, CUT INTO 1-INCH CUBES

3 CUPS DICED WHITE ONIONS

3 JALAPEÑOS, SEEDED AND DICED

2 (16-OUNCE) CANS PEAR TOMATOES, DICED

2 (16-OUNCE) CANS TOMATO PURÉE

3 TABLESPOONS OREGANO

3 TABLESPOONS CUMIN

1/3 CUP DRIED NEW MEXICO GREEN CHILIES

1/3 CUP PASILLA CHILI PEPPER

CAYENNE PEPPER

3 TABLESPOONS CHOPPED GARLIC

2 TABLESPOONS SALT

3/4 CUP WATER

2 PINTS BASS ALE

1 1/4 TABLESPOONS LEMON JUICE

FOR GARNISH:

2 CUPS SOUR CREAM

2 CUPS CHOPPED ONION

2 CUPS SHREDDED SHARP CHEDDAR CHEESE

CORN MUFFINS
(SEE RECIPE ON FACING PAGE)

1. In a large sauté pan, cook the bacon until crisp. Reserve the bacon and the melted fat separately.

2. In the same sauté pan, sauté as much of the diced pork butt as can fit in the pan, with 2 tablespoons of the peanut oil and about 1/3 of the bacon fat.

3. When the pork is browned, remove it from the oil and reserve with the bacon. Add another batch of pork to the pan, and cook in a similar fashion, continuing until all of the pork is cooked. When the oil/fat mixture becomes dark, discard it and add another portion of the peanut oil and reserved bacon fat.

4. When all of the pork is cooked, cook the sirloin using the same method.

5. In a large stockpot, combine the cooked bacon, pork and sirloin and any remaining peanut oil. Add the onion and jalapeños and sauté until the onion is transparent, about 5 minutes.

6. Add the tomatoes and tomato purée, oregano, cumin, green chilies, pasilla chili pepper, cayenne pepper, garlic, salt, water, Bass ale, and lemon juice. Bring to a boil, reduce heat, and simmer, covered, for 1 hour, until the meat is tender.

7. Serve hot, offering sour cream, chopped onion, sour cream, and Cheddar cheese as toppings, and Corn Muffins on the side.

Serving Size: 20

Venice Family Clinic Art Walk – "Kicking Ass at the Art Walk"
72 MARKET ST. CHILI AND CORN MUFFINS
photographed by Christine Caldwell

This dish may be cooked completely, chilled, then reheated the following day. You'll find preparing the Osso Buco in advance creates a thicker, richer flavor. But be careful not to overcook it when reheating, as the meat will become dry and stringy.

6 VEAL SHANKS

SALT AND PEPPER

1/2 CUP ALL-PURPOSE FLOUR

2 TABLESPOONS OLIVE OIL

2 CARROTS, FINELY DICED

1 MEDIUM ONION, FINELY DICED

2 CELERY STALKS, FINELY DICED

2 WHOLE GARLIC CLOVES

2 TEASPOONS CHOPPED THYME

1 BAY LEAF

1 CUP WHITE WINE

4 CUPS WATER

1 TABLESPOON TOMATO PASTE

1/2 TEASPOON PEPPER

1 TABLESPOON CHOPPED CHIVES

1. Preheat the oven to 375 degrees.

2. Season the veal shanks with salt and pepper and dust with flour. Reserve remaining flour.

3. Heat the oil in a sauté pan and sear the veal shanks until browned on both sides, about one minute each. Transfer to an ovenproof casserole.

4. In the same sauté pan, add the carrot, onion, celery, garlic, thyme, and bay leaf, and sauté for 5 minutes. Add to the casserole with the veal shanks.

5. Deglaze the sauté pan by adding the white wine and swirling the pan to loosen the remaining caramelized vegetables. Then pour the liquid onto the veal shanks.

6. In a small bowl, combine the remaining flour, water, tomato paste, and pepper, and add to the casserole and bring to a simmer on top of the stove.

7. Place the casserole in the oven and bake, covered, at 375 degrees for 1 hour.

8. To serve, remove the veal shank from casserole dish and spoon the sauce on top of it. Garnish with chopped chives.

Serving Size: 6

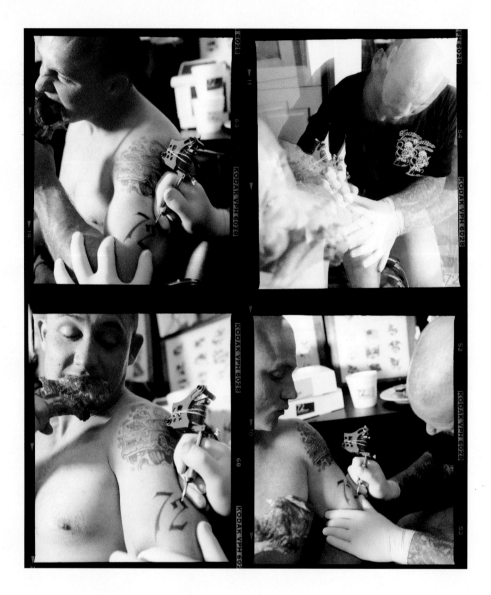

Andy Nevill, Tattoo Artist, and Mark Steffen, Actor - "Tattoo To Go"
VEAL CHOP WITH PORCINI MUSHROOMS AND SWEET POTATO PURÉE
photographed by Christine Caldwell

A simple but impressive dish. The sweetness of the purée is a subtle counterpoint to the earthy taste of the porcini mushrooms, but neither will overwhelm the delicate flavor of the veal. If you can't find demi-glace in your market, e-mail or fax us and we will send you a recipe.

1 CUP DRIED PORCINI MUSHROOMS

1 CUP HOT WATER

3 MEDIUM SWEET POTATOES,
PEELED AND DICED

4 CUPS WATER

SALT

2 TABLESPOONS PLUS 1 TEASPOON BUTTER

2 TABLESPOONS CHOPPED SHALLOTS

1 CUP RED WINE

1 CUP DEMI-GLACE

4 VEAL CHOPS

1/2 CUP WHIPPING CREAM

SALT AND PEPPER

1. Preheat the oven to 375 degrees.

2. Soak the dried porcini mushrooms in 1 cup of hot water and set aside.

3. Place the sweet potatoes in a large stockpot and cover with 4 cups water. Season with salt and bring to a boil. Cook until soft. Set aside.

4. Trim any fat off of the veal chops and discard. Season with salt, and set aside.

5. In a saucepan, heat 1 tablespoon of the butter. Add the shallots and sauté until they are translucent. Add the red wine and simmer, uncovered, until it is reduced by half.

6. Strain the porcini mushrooms, reserving both the liquid and the mushrooms. Add the strained water to the saucepan, and reduce by one-half. Add the demi-glace and reduce the heat to low.

7. In another pan, heat 1 teaspoon of the butter. Sauté the veal chops for 2 minutes on each side, or until browned. Place the meat in an ovenproof casserole and cook at 375 degrees for an additional 10 minutes.

8. While the meat is cooking, strain the sweet potatoes, reserving 1/2 cup of the liquid. Push the potatoes through a ricer and place in a mixing bowl with the cream and the remaining 1 tablespoon of butter. Season with salt and pepper to taste. Add a little of the reserved cooking liquid if you prefer a thinner purée.

9. When the sauce is thickened to the consistency of gravy, add the porcini mushrooms to it and check the seasoning.

10. Remove the veal from the oven and transfer to serving plates. Serve with the sweet potato purée, and top both the meat and potatoes with the porcini mushroom sauce, or serve the sauce on the side.

Serving Size: 4

Sweetbread and Lobster Chartreuse with Pea Coulis

1 CALF SWEETBREAD, VERY WHITE

SALT

CAYENNE PEPPER

2 EGGS

1 CUP WHIPPING CREAM

4 PARSNIPS

4 CARROTS

2$^{1}/_{2}$ TABLESPOONS BUTTER

1 Wash the sweetbread thoroughly in cold running water and place in a saucepan. Cover with water and bring to a boil. Boil for 3 minutes.

2 Remove the sweetbread from the water and place in a pan of ice water. When it is cool, remove the thin outer skin and the fat. Set aside.

3 In a food processor, purée 4 ounces (about half) of the sweetbread. Season with salt and cayenne.

4 Add the eggs and $^{1}/_{2}$ cup of the cream. Pulse until the mixture is puréed. Set aside.

5 With a vegetable peeler, peel the parsnips and carrots into long strips. Blanch separately by adding to a pot of boiling water. Return the pot to a boil, then immediately remove from the heat and strain the vegetables under cold water.

6 Butter six 8-ounce soufflé dishes (or chartreuse molds) using 1 tablespoon of the butter. Arrange the carrot and parsnip strips in alternating overlapping rows to cover the bottom and sides of the dishes.

7 Divide purée into six portions and spread one portion in each of the soufflé dishes. Cover and chill until ready to use.

Continued on next page

Sweetbread and Lobster Chartreuse with Pea Coulis

2 COOKED LOBSTERS IN THEIR SHELLS,
1 1/2 POUNDS EACH

2 TEASPOONS OLIVE OIL

3 SHALLOTS, SLICED VERY THIN

1 GARLIC CLOVE, SLICED VERY THIN

1 1/2 OUNCES COGNAC

1 1/2 CUPS WHITE WINE

1 BUNCH THYME, CHOPPED

2 TOMATOES, PEELED,
SEEDED AND CHOPPED

1/4 BUNCH TARRAGON, CHOPPED

1 BAY LEAF

SALT

CAYENNE PEPPER

1 CUP COOKED PEAS

Continued

8   Slice the lobster tail meat and remove the cartilage from the claws, saving the shells and the carcass. In a sauté pan, heat the olive oil. Add the shells and carcass of the lobster and sauté until they start to turn red, about 5 minutes.

9   Add 2 tablespoons of the chopped shallots and the garlic, and sauté for 5 minutes. Remove the excess oil.

10 Add the Cognac and 3/4 cup of the white wine. Bring to a simmer, then add the thyme, tomato, tarragon, and bay leaf, and season with salt and cayenne to taste. Cover and bring to a full boil, then reduce heat and simmer until the liquid is reduced by one-half. Strain and keep warm.

11 To make the pea coulis: Sauté the remaining shallots in 1/2 tablespoon butter until translucent. Add the rest of the wine and simmer until it is reduced by one-half. Add the peas and return to a boil. Add the remaining 1/2 cup of cream and return to a boil. Then remove from heat. Season with salt and cayenne. Purée in food processor, and keep warm.

12 Preheat oven to 350 degrees.

13 Heat 1 tablespoon of the butter in a sauté pan. Add the remaining sweetbread and sauté until golden, about 3 minutes on each side. Transfer to an ovenproof baking dish, and bake uncovered, at 350 degrees for 5 to 7 minutes.

14 Slice the sweetbread and combine with the sliced lobster tail meat. Add to the reserved lobster sauce and simmer for 2 minutes. Divide this mixture evenly among the six soufflé dishes.

15 Place the filled dishes and the reserved lobster claws in an ovenproof pan filled with hot water. Cover and let steam for 5 minutes on top of the stove or in a 350-degree oven.

16 Unmold onto serving plates. Drizzle the pea coulis around the chartreuses and garnish each with a lobster claw.

Serving Size: 6

Bear - "I've got a bone to pick . . ."
GRILLED PORK CHOP WITH TOMATO GINGER CHUTNEY
photographed by Gillian Lefcowitz

Pork goes well with assertive flavors, spices, acids and sweetness, so the Tomato Chutney is an
excellent partner. Today's pork is raised to be much leaner than in the past, so it's fine to serve
it cooked medium or medium well-done. The double cut chops make a handsome presentation.

Grilled Pork Chop with Tomato Ginger Chutney

FOR THE CHUTNEY:

¹/4 CUP DISTILLED WHITE VINEGAR

2 TABLESPOONS SUGAR

2 TEASPOONS FRESH GINGER,
VERY FINELY DICED

2 GARLIC CLOVES, FINELY CHOPPED

12 ROMA TOMATOES, PEELED,
SEEDED AND DICED

1 TEASPOON LEMON JUICE

¹/2 TEASPOON SALT

¹/2 TEASPOON PAPRIKA

¹/4 TEASPOON CAYENNE PEPPER

¹/4 TEASPOON DRY MUSTARD

PINCH OF GROUND CLOVES

6 DOUBLE CUT PORK CHOPS

SALT AND PEPPER

1   For the chutney: In a saucepan, heat the vinegar with the sugar, ginger, and garlic. Add the tomato, lemon juice, salt, paprika, cayenne, dry mustard, and ground cloves. Simmer for 15 to 20 minutes, or until most of liquid has evaporated. Reserve.

2   For the pork chops: Season pork chops with salt and pepper, and grill over medium-high heat for 7 to 10 minutes, or until cooked as desired. Serve with the Tomato Ginger Chutney on the side.

Serving Size: 6

We find domestic lamb is the most flavorful. It may have a bit more fat, but since you will be trimming the fat off the rack for this dish, we encourage you to use it. When you purchase the racks, make sure your butcher removes the chine and cracks between the ribs, so that it can be easily sliced into chops when serving.

Roasted Rack of Lamb with Orange and Juniper Berry Crust

RACK OF LAMB, ABOUT 3 POUNDS

2 TEASPOONS BUTTER

1 MEDIUM CARROT, DICED

1 MEDIUM ONION, DICED

1 CELERY STALK, DICED

1 GARLIC CLOVE

1 BAY LEAF

1 SPRIG THYME

2 TEASPOONS ORANGE ZEST,
CUT IN JULIENNE

2 TABLESPOONS SUGAR

1/4 CUP WATER

2 TEASPOONS ALMOND MEAL (OPTIONAL)

2 TEASPOONS PREPARED BREADCRUMBS

1 TEASPOON JUNIPER BERRIES

SALT AND PEPPER

1 Trim the fat from the lamb. Strip the meat and fat off the tips of the ribs. Discard the fat but retain the meat trimmings.

2 In a medium pan, melt 1 teaspoon of the butter and sauté the meat trimmings with the carrot, onion, celery, garlic, bay leaf, and thyme for about 7 minutes, or until evenly browned.

3 Cover with water, about 3 cups, and let simmer, uncovered, for 2 hours, skimming the fat from the top every 30 minutes. Strain and reserve. You should have about 6 ounces.

4 While the sauce is simmering, candy the orange zest by combining it with the sugar and water in a saucepan and bringing to a rolling boil. Cook until the mixture has the consistency of thick syrup, about 5 minutes. Do not let it become brown. Remove from heat.

5 Preheat the oven to 325 degrees. Remove the peels from the syrup and rinse lightly. Spread on a cookie sheet and bake for 5 to 10 minutes, until they are brittle but not browned. Cool.

6 Set candied peels between two sheets of wax paper and crush with a mallet or small hammer.

Continued on next page

Roasted Rack of Lamb with Orange and Juniper Berry Crust

Continued

7 In the bowl of a food processor, combine the candied orange zest with the almond meal and the breadcrumbs. Mix until combined, then add the juniper berries, pulsing the mixture a few times until combined.

8 Raise the oven temperature to 375 degrees.

9 Season the rack of lamb and rub it with some of the orange juniper mixture. Be sure to cover the entire rack of lamb, but do not pack it on. Roast for 20 minutes.

10 Remove the lamb from the oven and now, carefully pack on the remaining orange juniper mixture. Return to the oven for 10 minutes to finish cooking. Remove from the oven and let stand for 5 minutes before serving.

11 While the meat is resting, heat the sauce and season with salt and pepper to taste. Finish with 1 teaspoon of butter.

12 Slice the lamb and drizzle the sauce over the top. Serve immediately.

Serving Size: 4

Desserts

Julie Gibert, "Sweet Dreams" 140

63 Apple Galette with Caramel Sauce 141

64 Venice Banana Napoleon 142

Roy Doumani, "Why Men Have Mustaches" 144

65 72 Market St. Brownies 145

Carol Doumani, "Dressed to Spill" 146

66 Chocolate Hazelnut Torte 147

67 Pecan Pie 149

*Peter Sargent, Greg Berman
and David Vostmyer, "Just Desserts"* 150

68 Chocolate Crème Caramel 151

69 Lemon Meringue Tart 153

Michael Schiffer, "Chow Hound" 154

70 Cheesecake with Raspberry Coulis 155

Robert Lia, "Food for Thought" 156

71 Summer Pudding 157

72 Chocolate "Bombe" 158

Roland Gibert, "Bombe Scare" 160

Julie Gibert - "Sweet Dreams"
APPLE GALETTE WITH CARAMEL SAUCE
photographed by Randolph Dickerson

Granny Smith apples give this delicious dessert an edge of tartness to balance the sweetness of the caramel, but you may use other types of apples if you prefer. This recipe makes more than an ample amount of caramel sauce — chill or freeze what's left for future use.

Apple Galette with Caramel Sauce

FOR THE FILLING:

2 GRANNY SMITH APPLES,
PEELED, CORED AND DICED

1 TABLESPOON BUTTER

2 TABLESPOONS SUGAR

1 TABLESPOON WATER

1 TEASPOON CINNAMON

FOR THE GALETTE:

PUFF PASTRY SHEETS

2 GRANNY SMITH APPLES,
PEELED, CORED AND SLICED VERY THIN

1 TEASPOON SUGAR

1/2 TEASPOON CINNAMON

2 TEASPOONS BUTTER

CARAMEL SAUCE
(SEE RECIPE ON PAGE 143)

1. Preheat the oven to 350 degrees.

2. For the apple filling: Place the diced apples, 2 tablespoons sugar, 1 tablespoon butter, water, and 1 teaspoon cinnamon in a sauté pan. Cook, uncovered, over low heat, for 10 minutes, or until most of the water has evaporated. (Can be prepared ahead, covered, and chilled until ready to use.)

3. Cut the pastry sheets into four 4-inch circles. Place the pastry circles on a nonstick cookie sheet. Spoon about 1 tablespoon of the cooked apple into the center of each pastry circle.

4. Layer the sliced apple in a spiral pattern on top of the cooked apple, keeping it 1/4 inch from the edge of the pastry circle.

5. In a sauté pan, melt 2 teaspoons butter and add 1 teaspoon sugar and 1/2 teaspoon cinnamon.

6. Brush the galettes with the melted butter mixture, and bake at 350 degrees for 25 minutes, or until golden brown. Serve warm with Caramel Sauce.

Serving Size: 4

Venice Banana Napoleon

1 BOX PUFF PASTRY SHEETS, THAWED

CRÈME BRÛLÉE
(SEE RECIPE ON FACING PAGE)

CARAMEL SAUCE
(SEE RECIPE ON FACING PAGE)

CARAMELIZED BANANA
(SEE RECIPE ON FACING PAGE)

1 CUP POWDERED SUGAR

1. Prepare the Crème Brûlée and chill.

2. Prepare the Caramel Sauce and reserve at room temperature.

3. Prepare the Caramelized Banana and reserve at room temperature.

4. To make the napoleon fingers: Preheat the oven to 350 degrees. Cut the puff pastry sheets into eighteen 1-ounce portions, and roll each portion into a ball. Dust a flat surface with some of the powdered sugar and with a rolling pin, roll each ball into a thin finger about 5 inches long and 2 inches wide. Bake for 15 minutes, or until brown and crisp.

5. To assemble: Place one napoleon finger on a plate. Cover it with Crème Brûlée. Next, add a layer of Caramelized Banana. Repeat all three steps, and top with a napoleon finger. Garnish the plate with additional banana or other fresh fruit, and top with Caramel Sauce. The finished napoleon should be about 2 inches tall.

Serving Size: 6

Crème Brûlée

1 1/2 CUPS WHIPPING CREAM

1 CUP MILK

1/2 VANILLA BEAN, OR 1 TEASPOON VANILLA

1/2 CUP SUGAR

3 EGG YOLKS

1 WHOLE EGG

1. Preheat the oven to 325 degrees.

2. In a saucepan, bring the cream, milk, and vanilla bean to a boil. Promptly remove the pan from the heat. Remove the vanilla bean.

3. With an electric mixer, cream the sugar with the egg yolks and the whole egg, beating until the mixture is a pale yellow color. Slowly add the cream and milk mixture to the egg and sugar mixture, whisking constantly.

4. Pour the batter into a 9-inch-square pan. Place the pan in a larger pan and pour 1/2-inch of hot water into the larger pan to create a water bath.

5. Bake at 325 degrees for 25 minutes. Remove from oven and chill.

Caramel Sauce

1 CUP SUGAR

1/2 CUP WATER

1 CUP WHIPPING CREAM

1 1/2 TABLESPOONS BUTTER

1. In a deep saucepan, bring the sugar and water to a boil. Reduce heat and simmer, uncovered, for 5 minutes, or until the liquid turns golden brown. Remove pan from heat.

2. Slowly add the cream and then the butter, whisking constantly. Let cool, and serve at room temperature.

Caramelized Banana

1 CUP SUGAR

1/2 CUP WATER

2 TABLESPOONS BUTTER

4 PEELED BANANAS

1. Combine the sugar and water in a deep saucepan and bring to a rolling boil. Reduce heat and simmer for 3 to 5 minutes, or until golden brown.

2. Carefully stir in the butter.

3. Cut the banana in half crosswise, then cut each half lengthwise into two pieces, to make a total of 16 long strips. Add the banana to the sugar mixture and remove the pan from heat.

4. Let cool to room temperature.

Roy Doumani, Financier – "Why Men Have Mustaches"
72 MARKET ST. BROWNIES
photographed by Danny Duchovny

Every chef has a favorite brownie recipe. This is ours. We serve our brownies topped
with homemade vanilla bean ice cream and chocolate sauce. You will probably want to
72 Market St. Brownies
double the recipe as they seem to disappear quickly.

4 OUNCES UNSWEETENED CHOCOLATE

8 OUNCES BITTERSWEET CHOCOLATE

6 TABLESPOONS BUTTER, CUT IN SIX PIECES

2 CUPS SUGAR

4 EGGS

1 1/2 TEASPOONS VANILLA

10 TABLESPOONS ALL-PURPOSE FLOUR

1 1/2 CUPS WALNUTS

1. Preheat the oven to 325 degrees.

2. In a double boiler, melt the unsweetened and bittersweet chocolate with the butter.

3. In a mixing bowl, combine the sugar, eggs, vanilla, and flour.

4. Slowly add the chocolate mixture and mix until thoroughly incorporated.

5. Break the walnuts by hand into large pieces and add to the brownie batter.

6. Turn brownie batter into a nonstick or lightly buttered 9-inch-square pan. Bake at 325 degrees for 25 to 30 minutes, or until the center is firm and the brownies are beginning to pull away from the sides of the pan.

Serving Size: 9 to 12

Carol Doumani, Publisher – "Dressed to Spill"
CHOCOLATE HAZELNUT TORTE
photographed by Danny Duchovny

This wonderful recipe calls for three different types of chocolate, including Gianduja, a creamy mixture of toasted ground almonds, hazelnuts and chocolate. If you cannot find it in a specialty market, substitute milk chocolate.

Chocolate Hazelnut Torte

1 1/2 TABLESPOONS BUTTER

1/2 CUP SUGAR

1/3 CUP LOOSELY PACKED BROWN SUGAR

1/2 CUP ORANGE JUICE

1 1/2 TABLESPOONS FINELY CHOPPED HAZELNUTS

1 1/2 TABLESPOONS FINELY CHOPPED PISTACHIO NUTS

1/2 CUP ALL-PURPOSE FLOUR

4 OUNCES SEMISWEET CHOCOLATE

1 CUP PLUS 1/4 CUP WHIPPING CREAM

4 OUNCES MILK CHOCOLATE

4 OUNCES GIANDUJA CHOCOLATE

1 Using the paddle attachment of an electric mixer, beat the butter, sugar, and brown sugar until creamed, about 3 minutes.

2 Add the orange juice and chopped nuts, and mix until thoroughly incorporated.

3 With the mixer on slow speed, add the flour and mix well.

4 Preheat the oven to 325 degrees.

5 Carefully drop spoonfuls of the batter onto a greased cookie sheet, spreading into 4-inch circles. You will need to make 16 of these. Bake at 325 degrees for 10 minutes, until golden brown. Remove the cookies from the oven, and while they are still hot, press a 4-inch ring into each cookie and trim away the excess, to make the cookies uniform in shape. They should have the consistency of Florentines, flat, lacy, and chewy.

6 Melt the semisweet chocolate in the top of a double boiler.

7 In a separate saucepan, heat 1/4 cup of cream until it boils, then add it to the chocolate. Whisk together thoroughly.

8 While the cookies are still on the cookie sheet, carefully spread the chocolate on top of 8 of them.

9 Heat the milk chocolate and Gianduja chocolate together in the top of a double boiler.

10 In a separate saucepan, heat the remaining 1 cup cream until it boils, then add it to the Gianduja chocolate. Whisk together, then beat this mixture with an electric mixer until it cools and is the consistency of mousse. Pipe it on top of the 8 cookies covered with chocolate.

11 Top with the 8 leftover cookies. Chill until ready to serve.

Serving Size: 8

Many people are intimidated by pie crusts. Don't be — this recipe should be foolproof.

Pie Crust

1 ½ CUPS ALL-PURPOSE FLOUR

1 TABLESPOON SUGAR

PINCH OF SALT

4 TABLESPOONS UNSALTED BUTTER,
CUT INTO FOUR PIECES

2 EGG YOLKS

4 TABLESPOONS ICE WATER

¼ TEASPOON ALMOND EXTRACT
(OPTIONAL)

1   Preheat the oven to 350 degrees.

2   Combine the flour, sugar, and salt in a food processor fitted with a steel blade, and pulse several times.

3   Add the butter and pulse until the mixture resembles coarse meal.

4   While the processor is running, add the egg yolks, ice water, and almond extract through the feed tube, processing until the dough pulls away from the sides of the bowl and begins to form into a ball.

5   Remove the dough from the processor and wrap it in plastic. Chill at least one hour.

6   Roll out the dough between two sheets of wax paper, or on a flat surface dusted with flour, until it is large enough to fit a 10-inch pie pan. The dough should be about $^3/_8$-inch thick.

7   Carefully transfer the dough into the pie pan. Trim the excess dough and crimp the edges with a fork to form a decorative crust.

8   Using a fork, poke holes in the sides and bottom of the crust, line with aluminum foil, and fill with pie weights or dry beans or rice.

9   Bake at 350 degrees for 7 to 8 minutes, or until firm but not browned.

An all-American favorite refined with the taste of maple syrup. Be sure to purchase unsalted pecans rather than salted. The best variety comes from Georgia.

Pecan Pie

4 EGGS

¾ CUP MAPLE SYRUP

1 TEASPOON VANILLA

1 CUP BROWN SUGAR, PACKED

½ CUP UNSALTED BUTTER

2 CUPS PECANS, CHOPPED

10 PECAN HALVES, FOR DECORATION

WHIPPED CREAM, OR ICE CREAM

10-INCH PIE CRUST
(SEE RECIPE ON FACING PAGE)

1. Preheat the oven to 350 degrees.

2. Combine the eggs, maple syrup, and vanilla in a medium mixing bowl, and whisk until slightly thickened and pale gold in color.

3. Combine the brown sugar and butter in a small saucepan and cook over medium heat, whisking constantly, until the butter is melted. Let boil for 1 minute until slightly thickened.

4. Add the butter mixture to the egg mixture, stirring until blended.

5. Place the chopped pecans into a prepared pie shell, and pour the filling over. Decorate the top of the pie by placing pecans halves around the edge.

6. Bake at 350 degrees for 50 to 60 minutes, or until firm to the touch. Let cool. Serve at room temperature with a dollop of whipped cream or a scoop of ice cream.

Serving Size: 8

David Vostmyer, Peter Sargent, and Greg Berman, Art Directors – "Just Desserts"
CHOCOLATE CREME CARAMEL
photographed by Michael Cullen

Chocolate Crème Caramel

5 TABLESPOONS SUGAR

1/2 CUP WATER

2 CUPS MILK

1 CUP WHIPPING CREAM

4 EGGS

4 OUNCES SEMISWEET CHOCOLATE

WHIPPED CREAM

STRAWBERRIES, RASPBERRIES, OR BLUEBERRIES

1. Preheat the oven to 325 degrees.

2. In a saucepan, combine 1 tablespoon of the sugar and water, and boil for 5 minutes, until it caramelizes and is medium brown in color. Pour the sugar syrup into a 10-inch cake pan or casserole dish.

3. Rinse the saucepan and return to the stove. Heat the milk, cream and the rest of the sugar and bring to a boil. Remove the pan from the heat.

4. Break the eggs into a small bowl. Pour half of the milk mixture into the eggs, mixing slowly. Then pour this mixture back into the milk, whisking constantly.

5. In a double boiler, melt the chocolate. Add the cream and egg mixture and whisk until smooth.

6. Pour the mixture into the cake pan with sugar syrup in the bottom. Put the cake pan into a larger pan of warm water and bake at 325 degrees for 30 minutes or until firm.

7. Chill for 2 hours and unmold onto a 15-inch serving dish. Serve with whipped cream and berries or other fresh fruit.

Serving Size: 6

Pastry Shell

1/2 CUP SUGAR

2 EGGS

3 CUPS ALL-PURPOSE FLOUR

6 TABLESPOONS BUTTER

1/2 TEASPOON VANILLA EXTRACT

1. Using the paddle attachment of an electric mixer, combine the sugar, eggs, and flour.

2. With the mixer on medium speed, add the butter, 1 tablespoon at a time.

3. Add the vanilla, then gather the dough into a ball and cover with plastic. Chill for at least one hour.

4. Preheat the oven to 325 degrees.

5. On a floured surface, roll out dough to a thickness of $1/8$ inch. Transfer to a 9-inch tart pan, preferably one with a removable bottom. Prick the bottom and sides of the shell with a fork. Line the shell with aluminum foil and fill it with pie weights or dried beans or rice

6. Bake at 325 degrees for 15 minutes. Remove the foil and weights and continue baking until lightly browned, about 5 minutes.

Lemon Meringue Tart

4 EGG YOLKS, SEPARATED

2 WHOLE EGGS

1 CUP SUGAR

1 CUP FRESH LEMON JUICE

ZEST OF **3** LEMONS, CHOPPED FINE

1 TABLESPOON BUTTER

1/2 CUP SUGAR

1 DROP FRESH LEMON JUICE

1 PINCH OF SALT

9-INCH PASTRY SHELL, BAKED
(SEE RECIPE ON FACING PAGE)

1 In a double boiler, combine the egg yolks and whole eggs, sugar, lemon juice, and lemon zest, and cook for 12 to 15 minutes, or until the mixture becomes custard-like, whisking constantly.

2 Whisk in the butter. Cover and chill at least 1 hour.

3 While lemon filling is chilling, prepare the meringue by beating together the egg whites, 1/2 cup sugar, a drop of lemon juice, and a pinch of salt, until stiff peaks form.

4 Preheat the oven to 350 degrees.

5 Pour the lemon filling into the prepared pastry shell and top with the meringue. Bake at 350 degrees for 5 minutes, or until the meringue is lightly browned. Chill and serve.

Serving Size: 8

Michael Schiffer, Producer/Screenwriter - "Chow Hound"
LEMON MERINGUE TART
photographed by Danny Duchovny

One of our regular patrons likes to top his cheesecake with hot fudge, but fresh berries or
our Raspberry Coulis make delicious and colorful toppings which are a bit less decadent.

Cheesecake

2 CUPS GRAHAM CRACKER CRUMBS

1/2 CUP BROWN SUGAR, PACKED

16 TABLESPOONS BUTTER, SOFTENED

2 POUNDS CREAM CHEESE, SOFTENED

1/2 CUP SUGAR

1/2 TEASPOON SALT

2 TABLESPOONS LEMON JUICE

4 EGGS

1 To prepare the crust: Combine the graham cracker crumbs, brown sugar, and butter in a mixing bowl or food processor; mix on high speed until thoroughly incorporated. Press the mixture firmly into the bottom and sides of a 10-inch springform pan. Chill or freeze until ready to use.

2 For the filling: In a mixing bowl, beat the cream cheese on high until smooth. Add the sugar, salt, and lemon juice, and mix for 3 more minutes on high, or until smooth. Slowly add the eggs one at a time, beating until well mixed, about 5 minutes.

3 Preheat the oven to 325 degrees.

4 Pour the filling into the prepared crust. Place the spring-form pan in a larger pan filled with warm water and bake for 45 minutes or until set. Chill overnight. Serve with Raspberry Coulis.

Serving Size: 12

Raspberry Coulis

1 CUP WATER

1/2 CUP SUGAR

1 PINT BASKET FRESH RASPBERRIES, WASHED

1 Combine water, sugar and raspberries in a saucepan, and bring to a boil . Reduce heat to a simmer and cook, covered, for 2 to 3 minutes, stirring to blend thoroughly.

2 Press through a fine sieve to eliminate raspberry seeds. Chill and serve with slices of the cheesecake.

Serving Size: 12

Robert Lia, Chef - "Food for Thought"
SUMMER PUDDING
photographed by Pablo Aguilar

Bread pudding no doubt began as a way to use up leftover bread, a homey dish spooned onto a plate. This is a much more elegant version, the perfect finale to a summer meal. The fruit preserves add flavor to the recipe and the pectin in the preserves binds the berries together. Be sure to chill overnight before serving.

Summer Pudding

1 PINT BASKET OF FRESH RASPBERRIES

1 PINT BASKET OF FRESH BLUEBERRIES

1 PINT BASKET OF FRESH BLACKBERRIES

1 CUP SUGAR

1/2 CUP ORANGE JUICE

1/2 CUP APRICOT OR OTHER FRUIT PRESERVES

ZEST OF 1 ORANGE

ZEST OF 1 LEMON

18 SLICES WHITE BREAD

1 Clean the raspberries, blueberries, and blackberries.

2 In a saucepan, combine the whole berries with the sugar, orange juice, preserves, and zest. Bring the mixture to a boil, then reduce the heat and simmer, uncovered, for 5 minutes. Strain and reserve both the pulp and the strained liquid.

3 Cut the bread into twelve 4-inch circles. Place one circle in the bottom of each of six 4-ounce soufflé dishes. Cut rectangular pieces from the remainder of the bread and use them to line the insides of the soufflé dishes.

4 Pour the fruit and zest mixture into each soufflé dish. Top with another bread circle.

5 Pour the reserved fruit juice over each dish, using enough liquid to soak the bread. Cover with plastic, and chill overnight.

6 Unmold the chilled puddings onto serving plates and serve cold. Decorate with more juice or with Raspberry Coulis (see recipe on page 155) to make the plate more colorful.

Serving Size: 6

When your guests cut into these chocolate mousse cakes they will be rewarded with a flood of hot fudge oozing from the centers. The trick is in completely hiding the "explosion" within the batter so that the cake will cook around it. Also, take care when removing the pastry rings and the parchment paper from the cakes. If the surface is broken, the "explosion" will occur before the bombe gets to your guests!

Chocolate "Bombe"

FOR THE CHOCOLATE "EXPLOSION":

MELTED BUTTER

7 OUNCES WHIPPING CREAM

4 TABLESPOONS BUTTER, SOFTENED

8 OUNCES BITTERSWEET CHOCOLATE, MELTED

5 TABLESPOONS WATER

FOR THE MINT SAUCE:

1 HANDFUL FRESH MINT LEAVES

6 TABLESPOONS WATER

1 TEASPOON ARROWROOT

3/4 TEASPOON SUGAR

1 To prepare the rings: Cover a cookie sheet with parchment paper. Cut another piece of parchment paper or wax paper into six strips 4 inches high and 8 inches long. Brush them on one side with melted butter and encircle the insides of 6 individual pastry rings with the strips, butter side in, forming 4-inch-high cylinders. The melted butter will help the paper stick.

2 To prepare the "explosion": In a mixing bowl, whip the cream, butter, melted chocolate, and water. Grease a small loaf pan and line it with plastic wrap. Pour the mixture into it, cover, and freeze until hardened, about an hour.

3 To prepare the mint sauce: In a small saucepan, combine the mint and 5 tablespoons of the water, and bring to a boil. Remove from heat and let steep for several minutes, then remove the mint leaves.

4 In a small bowl, mix the arrowroot with the remaining 1 tablespoon water. Add this mixture to the mint tea. Add the sugar, and heat over a low flame until it melts. Set aside.

Continued on next page

Chocolate "Bombe"

FOR THE CHOCOLATE SYRUP:

3 TABLESPOONS SUGAR

7 TABLESPOONS WATER

2 TABLESPOONS COCOA POWDER

FOR THE CAKE:

2 EGGS, SEPARATED

3 TABLESPOONS SUGAR

1 TABLESPOON PLUS 1 TEASPOON CORNSTARCH

1 TABLESPOON PLUS 1 TEASPOON ALMOND MEAL

3 TABLESPOONS COCOA POWDER

1/2 PINCH OF SALT

FRESH MINT FOR GARNISH

Continued

5 To prepare the chocolate syrup: In a saucepan, combine the sugar and 1 tablespoon of the water, and cook over low heat until the sugar starts to caramelize and turn golden, approximately 5 minutes. Add the remaining 6 tablespoons of water to thin the caramel, then add the cocoa. Set aside until ready to use.

6 For the cake: In a mixing bowl, beat the egg yolks with the sugar until creamy. Add the cornstarch and almond meal, then add the cocoa. In another bowl, whip the egg whites with the salt until stiff peaks form, then fold them into the chocolate mixture. Transfer to a pastry bag.

7 To assemble: Preheat the oven to 350 degrees. Pipe the cake mixture into the prepared paper-lined rings, reserving a little to finish the cakes. Remove the chocolate "explosion" from the freezer and cut it into six pieces. The goal is to press a frozen explosion into the center of the cake batter so that it is completely covered. When you press down, be careful not to push it all the way to the bottom, so that the cake batter will cook all around it. Pipe more batter on top if necessary to fully cover the "explosions."

8 Bake the bombes for 14 minutes at 350 degrees. Remove from the oven and let cool for 5 minutes. Unmold by carefully slipping the rings off of the parchment-lined cakes. Then carefully unwrap the parchment from around the cakes. Use a spatula to transfer each cake onto a serving plate. Decorate with mint sauce, chocolate syrup, and fresh mint leaves if desired.

Serving Size: 6

Roland Gibert, Chef - "Bombe Scare"
CHOCOLATE "BOMBE"
photographed by Ronald Cadiz

Index

A

Aguilar, Pablo, 14, 22, 30, 96, 100, 110, 156

Air-Dried Duck, Crispy, with Pear and Mint Sauce, 119

Al, Wendy, 62

Aleiza and Lysandra, 46

Alexander, Peter, 48

Appetizer, 13-33 (See also Salad)
Artichoke and Asparagus Terrine with Beet Vinaigrette, 26
Ceviche, 21
Chicken Satay with Peanut Dipping Sauce, 33
Cod Fritters with Rouille, 19
Crab Cakes with Beluga Caviar, 15
Duck Spring Rolls with Orange Ginger Sauce, 29
Dungeness Crab and Crispy Noodle Galette with Spiced Mustard
    Sauce, 29
Onion and Cheddar Cheese Tart, 25
Prawns, Grilled with Japanese Vinaigrette, 17
Salmon, House-Cured, with Sauerkraut, 23
Veal Meatballs, 15

Apple(s)
Caramelized, Chicken with Calvados and, 113
Galette with Caramel Sauce, 141
Artichoke and Asparagus Terrine with Beet Vinaigrette, 26
Art Walk, 128

Asparagus
and Artichoke Terrine with Beet Vinaigrette, 26
Warm, with Carrot Tarragon Dressing, 75
Atil, Plaridel, ix, 61

B

Baerwald, David, 50

Banana
Caramelized, 143
Napoleon, Venice, 142
Squash Ravioli, 83
Bartlett, Helen, 114
Bean. See Black Bean; Fava Beans
Bear (the dog), 134

Beef
Chili and Corn Muffins, Kick Ass, 72 Market St., 127
Meat Loaf and Gravy, 72 Market St., 125
Beet Vinaigrette, 27

Bell Pepper (See also Pepper)
and Eggplant Terrine with Sun-Dried Tomato Vinaigrette, 72
Bengston, Billy Al, 62
Berman, Greg, 150
Berries, Summer Pudding, 157
Bill, Tony, ii, 114
Bisno, Leslie, 60
Bisque. See Soup
Black Bean Soup, 59
Bonner, Katherine, 36

Borgos, Gil, 14

Bouillabaisse, 72 Market St., 98-99

Brownies, 72 Market St., 145

C

Cadiz, Ronald, 46, 94, 120, 160

Calamari Salad, 45

Caldwell, Christine, 36, 82, 128, 130

Caramel Sauce, 143

Caramelized Banana, 143

Carrot Tarragon Dressing, 74

Cassel, Seymour, 32

Caviar, Beluga, Crab Cakes with, 31

Celery Root Mousse, 71

Ceviche, 21

Charred Peppered Rare Ahi Tuna with Sautéed Spinach and
    Red Onion Soubise, 97

Cheese, Cheddar, and Onion Tart, 25

Cheesecake with Raspberry Coulis, 155

Chicken, 111-15 (See also Duck; Quail; Squab)
with Caramelized Apples and Calvados, 113
Grilled Marinated, with Tomatillo Salsa, 111
Grilled, and Vegetables, Fettuccine with, and Red Pepper Pesto, 89
Salad, Chinese, 47
Satay with Peanut Dipping Sauce, 33
Stuffed with Tarragon Mousse in a Sea Urchin Sauce, 115

Chili and Corn Muffins, Kick Ass, 72 Market St., 127

Chinese Chicken Salad, 47

Chocolate
"Bombe," 158-59
Brownies, 72 Market St., 145
Crème Caramel, 151
Hazelnut Torte, 147

Chowder. (See also Soup)
Clam, Sweet Potato, 64
Corn, Spicy, 55
Chroman, Nate and Judy, 100
Clam Chowder, Sweet Potato, 64
Cod Fritters with Rouille, 19

Corn
Chowder, Spicy, 55
Muffins, 126

Crab
Cakes with Beluga Caviar, 31
Dungeness, and Crispy Noodle Galette with Spiced Mustard Sauce, 29
Crayfish Salad Wrapped in Smoked Salmon with Mango Vinaigrette, 37
Crème Brûlée, 143
Crème Caramel, Chocolate, 151
Cullen, Michael, 20, 62, 150

D

Danson, Ted, 54

DeAngelis, Joe, 104

Dessert, 141-58

Apple Galette with Caramel Sauce, 141
Banana Napoleon, Venice, 142
Brownies, 72 Market St., 145
Caramelized Banana, 143
Cheesecake with Raspberry Coulis, 155
Chocolate "Bombe," 158-59
Chocolate Créme Caramel, 151
Chocolate Hazelnut Torte, 147
Créme Brûlée, 143
Lemon Meringue Tart, 153; Pastry Shell for, 152
Pecan Pie, 149; Pie Crust for, 148
Summer Pudding (berries), 157

Dickerson, Randolph, 140, 167

Doumani, Carol, 146

Doumani, Roy, 144

Duchovny, Danny, ii, 32, 38, 60, 86, 104, 106, 114, 144, 146, 154

Duck

Crispy Air-Dried, with Pear and Mint Sauce, 119
Muscovy, with Port Wine Sauce, 118
Spring Rolls with Orange Ginger Sauce, 13

Dungeness, and Crispy Noodle Galette with Spiced Mustard Sauce, 29

E

Eggplant and Bell Pepper Terrine with Sun-Dried Tomato Vinaigrette, 72

Evans, James, 82

F

Fall Fruit Salad, 51

Farfalle Pasta with Fava Beans and Mushroom Ragout, 87

Fava Beans, Farfalle Pasta with, and Mushroom Ragout, 87

Fegan, Robert, 94

Fennel Ratatouille, 77

Ferguson, Steve, 112

Fettuccine with Grilled Chicken and Vegetables and Red Pepper Pesto, 89

Fish, 95-107 (See also Seafood)

Bouillabaisse, 72 Market St., 98-99
Ceviche (sea bass), 21
Cod Fritters with Rouille, 19
Halibut, Baked, with Wild Mushroom Crust and Lentil Ragout, 102-3
Papillote, 72 Market St. (red snapper), 107
Salmon, Grilled, with Dijon and Pommery Mustard Sauce, 95
Salmon with Sauerkraut, House-Cured, 23
Smoked Salmon, Crayfish Salad Wrapped in, with Mango Vinaigrette, 37
Tuna, Ahi, Charred Peppered Rare, with Sautéed Spinach and Red Onion Soubise, 97

Fong, Matt (The Honorable), and Paula Fong, 30

Fruit Salad, Fall, 51

G

Garlic, Candied, Roasted Squab with, and Green Lentil Ragout, 116-17

Gazpacho, 63

Gibert, Julie, 140

Gibert, Roland, ii, ix, 160

Gnocchi, Swiss Chard, with Sage Butter, 91

Grilled (See also Charred; Seared)

Marinated Chicken with Tomatillo Salsa, 111
Portobello Mushrooms and a Small Mesclun with Red Pepper Vinaigrette, 49
Prawns with Japanese Vinaigrette, 17
Salmon with Dijon and Pommery Mustard Sauce, 95
Seafood and Vegetable Salad with Lemon Vinaigrette, 43

Gumbo

Quail, Ed Landry's, 121
Seafood, with Rock Shrimp, 56

H

Halibut, Baked, with Wild Mushroom Crust and Lentil Ragout, 102-3

Herb Sauce, Lobster and Green Onion Ravioli with, 85

House-Cured Salmon with Sauerkraut, 23

J

Jacobucci, Sharon, 60

Japanese Vinaigrette, 16

K

Kallianiotes, Helena, 110

Katz, Marjorie, 100

Kay, Nancy, 44

Keller, Alexandra, 90

Kitchen, E.F., 44, 76

Kresl, Anne, 90

L

Lamb, Roasted Rack of, with Orange and Juniper Berry Crust, 136-37

(Ed) Landry's, Quail Gumbo, 121

Lefcowitz, Gillian, 48, 50, 54, 134

Lemon

Meringue Tart, 153; Pastry Shell for, 152
Vinaigrette, 42

Lentil

Green, Ragout, Roasted Squab with Candied Garlic and, 116-17
Ragout, Baked Halibut with Wild Mushroom Crust and, 102-3

Lia, Robert, 120, 156

Linn, Connie, 38

Lobster

Bisque, 57
and Green Onion Ravioli with Herb Sauce, 85
Napoleon, Maine, 39
and Sweetbread Chartreuse with Pea Coulis, 132-33

Lysandra and Aleiza, 46

M

Maine Lobster Napoleon, 39

Mango Vinaigrette, 39

Mauri Dough, Tart Shells from, 24

Meat. See also Beef; Lamb; Pork; Sweetbread; Veal Loaf and Gravy, 72 Market St., 125; Gravy, 124

Meatballs, Veal, 31

Mesclun, a Small, Grilled Portobello Mushrooms and, with Red Pepper Vinaigrette, 49

Miller, Peter Darley, 122

Moore, Dudley, ii, 86

Moses, Ed, 96

Mousse, Celery Root, 71

Muffins, Corn, 126

Muscovy Duck with Port Wine Sauce, 118

Mushroom(s)

Bisque, 58
Porcini, and Sweet Potato PurÇe, Veal Chop with, 131
Portobello, Grilled, and a Small Mesclun with Red Pepper Vinaigrette, 49
Ragout, Farfalle Pasta with Fava Beans and, 87
Wild, Crust, 103

Mustard Sauce

Dijon and Pommery, Grilled Salmon with, 95
Spiced, 28

N

Nevill, Andy, 130

Noodle Galette, Crispy, and Dungeness Crab, with Spiced Mustard Sauce, 29

O

Onion(s)

Caramelized, Seared Sea Scallops with, and Sweet and Sour Sauce, 101
and Cheddar Cheese Tart, 25
Orange Ginger Sauce, 12
Osso Buco, 129

P

Paella, 72 Market St., 105
Papillote, 72 Market St., 107
Parsnip Soup, Cream of, with Ginger, 65

Pasta, 83-91 (See also Risotto)

Farfalle, with Fava Beans and Mushroom Ragout, 87
Fettuccine with Grilled Chicken and Vegetables and Red Pepper Pesto, 89
Gnocchi, Swiss Chard, with Sage Butter, 91
Noodle Galette, Crispy, and Dungeness Crab, with Spiced Mustard Sauce, 29
Ravioli, Banana Squash, 83
Ravioli Dough, 84
Ravioli, Green Onion, Lobster and, with Herb Sauce, 85

Pastry Shell 152

Pea Coulis, Sweetbread and Lobster Chartreuse with, 132-33

Pear

and Mint Sauce, Crispy Air-Dried Duck with, 119
and Roquefort Torte, Warm, with Salad Greens and Red Wine Vinaigrette, 40
Pecan Pie, 149; Pie Crust for, 148

Pepper

Bell, and Eggplant Terrine with Sun-Dried Tomato Vinaigrette, 72
Red, Pesto, 88
Red, Vinaigrette, 49

Pesto, Red Pepper, 88

Pie, Pecan, 149; Crust for, 148

Porcini Mushrooms and Sweet Potato Purée, Veal Chop with, 131

Pork

Chili and Corn Muffins, Kick Ass, 72 Market St., 127
Sausage, Meat Loaf and Gravy, 72 Market St., 125
Portobello Mushrooms, Grilled, and a Small Mesclun with Red Pepper Vinaigrette, 49

Potatoes (See also Sweet Potato)

au Gratin, 70
Mashed, 72 Market St., 69

Prawns (See also Shrimp)

Grilled with Japanese Vinaigrette, 17

Q

Quail Gumbo, Ed Landry's, 121

R

Rack of Lamb, Roasted, with Orange and Juniper Berry Crust, 136-37

Raspberry Coulis, Cheesecake with, 155

Ratatouille, Fennel, 77

Ravioli

Banana Squash, 83
Dough, 84
Green Onion, Lobster and, with Herb Sauce, 85

Red Pepper (See also Pepper)

Pesto, 88
Vinaigrette, 49

Red snapper, Papillote, 72 Market St., 107

Red Wine Vinaigrette, 41

Risotto

Seafood, with Saffron, 81
Vegetable, 80
Rouille, 18

S

Sage Butter, Swiss Chard Gnocchi with, 91

Salad, 37-51

Calamari, 45
Chicken, Chinese, 47
Crayfish, Wrapped in Smoked Salmon with Mango Vinaigrette, 37
Fruit, Fall, 51
Greens, Warm Pear and Roquefort Tart with, and Red Wine Vinaigrette, 40
Grilled Seafood and Vegetable, with Lemon Vinaigrette, 43
Lobster Napoleon, Maine, 39
Mesclun, a Small, Grilled Portobello Mushrooms and, with Red Pepper Vinaigrette, 49

Salmon

Grilled, with Dijon and Pommery Mustard Sauce, 95
with Sauerkraut, House-Cured, 23
Smoked, Crayfish Salad Wrapped in, with Mango Vinaigrette, 37

Samakow, Daniel, 82

Sargent, Peter, 150

Sauce (See also Vinaigrette)

Caramel, 143
Carrot Tarragon Dressing, 74
Meat Loaf Gravy, 125

Mustard, Spiced, 28
  Orange Ginger, 12
  Red Pepper Pesto, 88
  Rouille, 18
Sauerkraut, House-Cured Salmon with, 23

Scallops
  Bay, Ceviche, 21
  Sea, Seared, with Caramelized Onions and Sweet and Sour Sauce, 101
Schiffer, Michael, 154
Schwartz, Leonard, 122
Sea bass, Ceviche, 21
Sea Urchin Sauce, Chicken Stuffed with Tarragon Mousse in a, 115

Seafood (See also Fish)
  Bouillabaisse, 72 Market St., 98-99
  Calamari Salad, 45
  Ceviche, 21
  Clam Chowder, Sweet Potato, 64
  Crab Cakes with Beluga Caviar, 31
  Crayfish Salad Wrapped in Smoked Salmon with Mango Vinaigrette, 37
  Dungeness Crab and Crispy Noodle Galette with Spiced Mustard Sauce, 29
  Gumbo with Rock Shrimp, 56
  Lobster. See Lobster
  Paella, 72 Market St., 105
  Papillote, 72 Market St., 107
  Prawns Grilled with Japanese Vinaigrette, 17
  Risotto with Saffron, 81
  Scallops, Sea, Seared, with Caramelized Onions and Sweet and Sour Sauce, 101
  Sea Urchin Sauce, Chicken Stuffed with Tarragon Mousse in a, 115
  and Vegetable Salad, Grilled, with Lemon Vinaigrette, 43
  Seared Sea Scallops with Caramelized Onions and Sweet and Sour Sauce, 101

72 Market St.
  Bouillabaisse, 98-99
  Brownies, 145
  Chili, Kick Ass, and Corn Muffins, 127
  Mashed Potatoes, 69
  Meat Loaf and Gravy, 125
  Paella, 105
  Papillote, 107

Shrimp (See also Prawns)
  Rock, Seafood Gumbo with, 56
Smoked Salmon, Crayfish Salad Wrapped in, with Mango Vinaigrette, 37

Soup, 55-65
  Black Bean, 59
  Clam Chowder, Sweet Potato, 64
  Corn Chowder, Spicy, 55
  Cream of Parsnip, with Ginger, 65
  Gazpacho, 63
  Lobster Bisque, 57
  Mushroom Bisque, 58
  Quail Gumbo, Ed Landry's, 121
  Seafood Gumbo with Rock Shrimp, 56
  Vegetable Split Pea, 61
Spinach, Sautéed, and Red Onion Soubise, Charred Peppered Rare Ahi Tuna with, 97
Split Pea Vegetable Soup, 61
Spring Rolls, Duck, with Orange Ginger Sauce, 13
Squab, Roasted, with Candied Garlic and Green Lentil Ragout, 116-17
Squash, Banana, Ravioli, 83

Steenburgen, Mary, 54
Steffen, Mark, 130
Stewart, Linda, 106
Summer Pudding (fresh berries), 157
Sun-Dried Tomato Vinaigrette, 73

Sweet Potato
  Clam Chowder, 64
  Purée and Porcini Mushrooms, Veal Chop with, 131
Sweet and Sour Sauce, Seared Sea Scallops with Caramelized Onions and, 101
Sweetbread and Lobster Chartreuse with Pea Coulis, 132-33
Swiss Chard Gnocchi with Sage Butter, 91

T

Tart
  Onion and Cheddar Cheese, 25
  Shells from Mauri Dough, 24
  Warm Pear and Roquefort, with Salad Greens and Red Wine Vinaigrette, 40

Terrine
  Artichoke and Asparagus, with Beet Vinaigrette, 26
  Eggplant and Bell Pepper, with Sun-Dried Tomato Vinaigrette, 72
Tomatillo Salsa, Grilled Marinated Chicken with, 111
Tomato. See Sun-Dried Tomato

Torte
  Chocolate Hazelnut, 147
  Warm Pear and Roquefort, with Salad Greens and Red Wine Vinaigrette, 40
Truax, Sharon, 76
Tuna, Ahi, Charred Peppered Rare, with Sautéed Spinach and Red Onion Soubise, 97
Turner, William, 20

V

Van Nimwegen, Derrik, 76

Veal
  Chop with Porcini Mushrooms and Sweet Potato Purée, 131
  Meatballs, 15
  Osso Buco, 129

Vegetable(s), 69-77 (See also Name of Vegetable)
  and Grilled Chicken, Fettuccine with, and Red Pepper Pesto, 89
  Risotto, 80
  and Seafood Salad, Grilled, with Lemon Vinaigrette, 43
  Split Pea Soup, 61
Venice Banana Napoleon, 142

Vinaigrette (See also Sauce)
  Beet, 27
  Japanese, 16
  Lemon, 42
  Mango, 39
  Red Pepper, 49
  Red Wine, 41
  Sun-Dried Tomato, 73
Vostmyer, David, 150

W

Wallace, Steve, 22
Waller, E.K., 112
Wild Mushroom Crust, 103

We gratefully acknowledge the photographers whose dazzling work illustrates this book.

Danny Duchovny

ii Tony Bill, Roland Gibert and Dudley Moore

32 Seymour Cassel, Actor .... *Up in Smoke*

38 Connie Linn, Patron .... *In Living Color*

60 Sharon Jacobucci, Metermaid and Leslie Bisno, Waiter .... *Meal Ticket*

86 Dudley Moore, Entertainer .... *Hitting the High Notes*

104 Joe DeAngelis, Mr. Universe and Mr. World .... *Pumping Paella*

106 Linda Stewart, Producer and Danny Duchovny, Director .... *Two Shot*

114 Helen Bartlett, Producer and Tony Bill, Director .... *Fowl Play*

144 Roy Doumani, Financier .... *Why Men Have Mustaches*

146 Carol Doumani, Publisher .... *Dressed to Spill*

154 Michael Schiffer, Producer/Screenwriter .... *Chow Hound*

Pablo Aguilar

14 Gil Borgos, Greeter .... *On a Roll*

22 Steve Wallace, Wine Merchant .... *Vintage Wally*

30 Matt Fong, Treasurer of the State of California, and Paula Fong .... *Party Politics*

96 Ed Moses, Painter .... *In Rare Form*

100 Nate and Judy Chroman, and Marjorie Katz, Wine Connoiseurs .... *The Last Supper*

110 Helena Kallianiotes, Impresario .... *Zesty*

156 Robert Lia, Chef .... *Food for Thought*

Ronald Cadiz

46 Aleiza and Lysandra .... *Chopstix*

94 Robert Fegan, Waiter .... *Catch of the Day*

120 Robert Lia, Chef, and Canoah .... *Main Squeeze*

160 Roland Gibert, Chef .... *Bombe Scare*

Christine Caldwell

36 Katherine Bonner, Photographer/Illustrator .... *The Little Mermaid*

82 James Evans and Daniel Samakow, Restaurateurs .... *Your Place or Ours?*

128 Venice Family Clinic Art Walk .... *Kicking Ass at the Art Walk*

130 Andy Nevill, Tattoo Artist and Mark Steffen, Actor .... *Tattoo To Go*

Gillian Lefcowitz

48 Peter Alexander, Artist .... *Lunch in the Abstract*

50 David Baerwald, Musician .... *After Hours*

54 Ted Danson and Mary Steenburgen, Actors .... *Soup du Jour*

134 Bear .... *I've got a bone to pick*

Michael Cullen

20 William Turner, Gallery Owner .... *Ceviche on the Canal*

62 Billy Al Bengston, Owner/Director of Billy's Studio, and Wendy Al .... *The First Time I Ever Liked Gazapacho*

150 David Vostmyer, Peter Sargent and Greg Berman, Art Directors .... *Just Desserts*

Plaridel Atil

ix ROLAND GIBERT

Randolph Dickerson

140 JULIE GIBERT .... Sweet Dreams
167 TABLE TOP .... Tip Not Included

E.F. Kitchen

44 NANCY KAY, ARTIST, AND E.F. KITCHEN, PHOTOGRAPHER WITH BORIS AND IGOR .... Photo Op
76 SHARON TRUAX, ART DEALER, AND DERRIK VAN NIMWEGEN, ARTIST .... Say Ahhh!

Robert Graham

68 SELF-PORTRAIT .... Self-Portrait in Mashed Potatoes

Anne Kresl

90 ALEXANDRA KELLER .... The Shortest Distance Beween Two Points Is a Straight Line

Peter Darley Miller

122 LEONARD SCHWARTZ, CHEF .... From Market St. to Maple Dr.

E.K. Waller

112 STEVE FERGUSON, PIANIST .... Concerto for Chicken and Apples
ALL FOOD INSETS

WE GRATEFULLY ACKNOWLEDGE THE HOME CHEFS WHO HELPED US TEST RECIPES:

MARY BRAHENY	DAVID GOLDHILL	JEAN PADBERG	ERNIE AND PAT SCHRODER
ROBERT FEGAN	CONNIE LINN	STUART PATTERSON	SANDY SINGER
EVELYN GIBERT	SUSAN MILLER	TOM ROACH	

And our copy editor:
ANGELINE VOGL

And our proof reader:
MARYLOU LIA

And our indexer:
ROSE GRANT

Food design by
ROBERT LIA

Designed by
DAVID VOSTMYER,
SARGENT & BERMAN, INC.

Printed By
C&C OFFSET PRINTING CO., LTD.

"Tip Not Included"
photographed by Randolph Dickerson